SPORTS AFIELD

Treasury of

WATERFOWL

SPORTS AFIELD

Treasury of
WATERFOWL

Paintings by Angus H. Shortt

Text by B. W. Cartwright

PRENTICE-HALL, INC.   ENGLEWOOD CLIFFS, N. J.

Originally Published Under the Title
KNOW YOUR DUCKS AND GEESE

© Copyright, 1948, 1957, by
SPORTS AFIELD MAGAZINE, INC.

LIBRARY OF CONGRESS CATALOG CARD NUMBER: 57-11975

PRINTED IN THE UNITED STATES OF AMERICA BY THE BUREAU OF ENGRAVING, INC.

83551

Dedicated to

WATERFOWLERS EVERYWHERE

FOREWORD

There is an adage in the magazine business that the surest way to sell copies of general interest publications is to run pictures of either babies or puppies. I don't know how true this is, but I do know that one of the surest appeals for an outdoor magazine is paintings of waterfowl. That is how *Sports Afield* Magazine came to commission Angus H. Shortt to do a series of paintings in full color on all the important ducks and geese of North America.

In addition to enjoying waterfowl pictures, readers are always eager to have as much descriptive information as possible about each species, so B. W. Cartwright was asked to supply an authoritative text to accompany each of Shortt's paintings. Angus Shortt is artist-technician of Ducks Unlimited (Canada), and Mr. Cartwright is chief naturalist for that organization. Both men live and work in Manitoba, the fountainhead of the continent's duck supply. They study ducks and geese 365 days each year.

This series proved extremely popular with the magazine's readers. Many wrote and asked for reprints, but unfortunately there were only a handful available. Many clipped the prints from the magazine, but they were eager to have something of a more permanent nature; and that is how this SPORTS AFIELD TREASURY OF WATERFOWL came to be made.

We don't know of any other volume in existence that contains as many fine paintings of the different varieties of North American waterfowl. It is designed not only for the enjoyment of the color plates, but as an easy reference, with a complete descriptive text and distribution map for the identification of each species of duck and goose. It is printed on heavy, high-grade lithographic stock by the finest process known, to insure fidelity of color and long life.

The colored illustrations in all instances depict the male and female of each species in full flight. The text carries black-and-white sketches of the birds on the water and a map showing the known distribution in North America. Special care has been taken to insure the reproduction of the natural colors with the utmost fidelity.

Cartwright's text gives the latest available information on the habits and distribution of each species. Much new knowledge has been incorporated. Great care has been taken to present only scientifically established facts, so that the text may be accepted as authoritative. The nomenclature used is that of the 20th Supplement to "The A.O.U. Check-list of North American Birds," *The Auk* (October, 1945), published by the American Ornithologists Union.

Basic reference works used are *Birds of Massachusetts and Other New England States*, by Edward Howe Forbush (1925); *Birds of Minnesota*, by Thomas S. Roberts (1932); *The Ducks, Geese and Swans of North America*, by Francis H. Kortright (1942) and various publications of the Illinois Natural History Survey. Other specialists who have been consulted are cited within the text of the book. The accumulated data of Ducks Unlimited (Canada) have been freely used, and its cooperation is gratefully acknowledged.

The illustrations show the ducks in the full nuptial plumage that ducks gradually assume in late fall, carry throughout the winter and spring and lose shortly after the advance of the breeding season. The males then molt and grow a plumage known as "eclipse plumage," which closely resembles that of the female. The wing feathers, renewed during this molt, are shed just once a year. The eclipse plumage lasts for two or three months, gradually changing until full nuptial plumage is again assumed. Considerable variation is shown by individuals of a species and among species in the times that these plumage changes begin and end. It was not practical to illustrate all these changes, but the characteristic markings of species in any plumage has been emphasized in the text so that identification may be established without doubt.

Throughout the text certain standard terms accepted by ornithologists may be unfamiliar to some sportsmen. These are defined as introduced, and consistently used. The use of scientific terms, however, has been held to a minimum. Descriptions are confined as far as possible to outstanding markings, habits, call notes or other peculiarities characteristic of the species under discussion. A special effort has been made to reduce the identification of ducks and geese to the simplest terms, so that sportsmen may be able to identify every specimen they see while in a blind and thus derive even greater interest from the sport that many believe to be the finest in the world.

There are two classes of ducks: the surface-feeders and the divers. The former, variously called pond ducks, river ducks, puddle ducks, dabblers and tip-up ducks, include such fine sporting species as the Mallard, Black Duck, Pintail, the various teals, the Baldpate, Gadwall, Shoveller and Wood Duck.

The divers, variously called sea or bay ducks and deep-water ducks, include the Canvasback, Redhead, Greater and Lesser Scaups (Bluebills), Ringneck (Blackjack), Goldeneye (Whistler), Bufflehead (Butterball), Harlequin, the eiders and scoters, the Ruddy Duck and the Merganser. When taking off from the water, surface-feeding ducks leap straight up into the air and get under way by sheer wing power. The divers patter along on the surface of the water for some distance to get up flying speed before they launch themselves into the air. (See sketches.)

Hence, by observing the type of take-off you can immediately classify the species you are looking at as surface-feeding or diving.

Surface-feeders have narrow lobes on the hind toe and divers have broad lobes. (See sketch.) Hence, in seeking to identify a

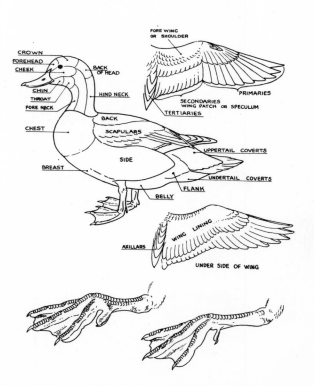

specimen in the hand, the kind of lobe on the hind toe serves at once to place it in one of the two groups.

The field having thus been narrowed, the next steps in identifying a species have to do with shapes, patterns and markings and can only be dealt with under each species. To remove any doubt as to what we may be talking about when referring to characteristic patterns or markings, Mr. Shortt has sketched a simple, topographical outline of a duck and its wing. (See sketch on page viii.)

TED KESTING
Editor
Sports Afield Magazine

CONTENTS

SPORTS AFIELD

Treasury of

WATERFOWL

BALDPATE

(American Widgeon[1])   (*Mareca americana*)

MALE   FEMALE

COMMON NAMES

Baldpate, Baldy, Widgeon.

DESCRIPTION

A medium-sized, handsome duck of the surface-feeding group. Breeds only in North America. Has increased remarkably in the last five years.

Adult male in flight. *A conspicuous white, oval-shaped patch on the forewing* is the most distinctive field mark of this species. The lower breast and belly are white. Wing linings white. Utters three or four musically whistled notes, which usually are twice repeated in rapid succession.

Adult male on water. Rides high, tail well up. Prominent *white forehead and crown* (from which the species gets its name)— creamy-buff in some individuals—is readily seen. Gray neck and brownish body. Tail end dark, with conspicuous white patch between tail and purplish-cinnamon sides. White streak on folded wing.

Adult female in flight. Similar to male but without white cap. *White* wing patches are prominent and distinctive.

Adult female on water. Gray head and neck, brownish body. *White under tail; white streak on folded wing.*

DISTRIBUTION

Baldpates nest more abundantly in western Canada than in any other part of their breeding range, which extends from Keewatin (Hudson Bay) west to northwestern Alaska, northern British Columbia, Washington, Oregon and northern California, Nevada, Utah, northern Colorado, Nebraska, Minnesota (probably), Wisconsin and northern Indiana. Rare breeder east of the Mississippi.

Winters from British Columbia south to Central America on the

---

[1] The European Widgeon (*M. penelope*) is frequently taken in fall and winter on the Atlantic coast from Newfoundland to the West Indies. Seven bands recovered in America were all from birds banded in Iceland. This suggests a regular migration from that island to this continent. (May Thatcher Cooke in *Bird Banding*, Vol. XVI, No. 4, Oct. 1945.) This species also is occasionally taken on the Pacific coast and more rarely in the interior. It is not known to nest on this continent.

Pacific slope, and from Massachusetts (rarely) and Chesapeake Bay south to the Lesser Antilles and Costa Rica. In the interior—from the midcontinent states south through Mexico.

NORTHWARD MIGRATION

The first Baldpates reach the western provinces of Canada early in April, often in company with Pintails; but the peak of the spring flight is in late April or early May. It depends largely on weather. Some pair after their arrival and dally along until late in May before settling down to nesting duties.

COURTSHIP AND NESTING

No more graceful, swifter, more recklessly erratic nuptial flights are seen than those of the Baldpates. They dart this way and that, up and down, with bewildering changes of direction. As with other species, a female may start out with a single male in pursuit and soon have a retinue of four to twelve suitors vying with each other for her favors. Excitedly calling with pleasantly musical whistles, the males try to get ahead of her to display their vigor and plumage.

On the water, the love-making is similar to that of the Gadwall and other species, consisting of much head-bobbing, endearing notes, sidling up to the female and bowing.

The nest is a grass-lined cavity, well concealed at the base of a willow, among coarse vegetation or back in the woods. Always on the ground and copiously walled around with gray down. The location may be near or quite some distance from water. Eggs are creamy-white, six to twelve in number—average 10.

Incubation period: about 23 days, by female only.

Brood counts in the last week of July, covering seven years, by Ducks Unlimited's keemen, gave a total of 8,774 females with 50,282 young—an average brood of 5.7.

FOOD

Baldpates are "hijackers." They often ride herd on Canvasbacks, Redheads and Whitebills (Coots), particularly in fall and winter. I have seen a pond covered with a scattering of Coots, with two or three Baldpates or Baldpates and Gadwalls in attendance on each Coot. Up would come the diver with pondweed trailing from his bill, and there would be a concerted rush to grab as much as possible by each of the poachers.

Ninety-three per cent of the Baldpate's food is vegetable matter—pondweeds (Potamogetons), grasses and algae by preference, which it finds in shallow ponds and secures by "tipping up." It is said to feed much at night. The balance of 7 per cent is made up of aquatic insects and mollusks.

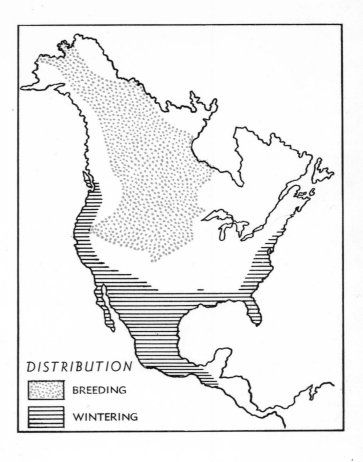

DISTRIBUTION

BREEDING

WINTERING

WEIGHTS[2]

Male—*Average of 12 adults:* 1.79 pounds. *Average of 87 juveniles:* 1.70 pounds.

Female—*Average of 15 adults:* 1.70 pounds. *Average of 93 juveniles:* 1.56 pounds.

SOUTHWARD MIGRATION

Baldpates start south from Canada about the third week of September and, except for a relatively few hardy ones, are mostly all gone by October 10. There is a heavy migration through Washington, Oregon and California, many staying to winter, and later to bring grief to the lettuce-growers in those states. In the interior, the main flights are through the central and Mississippi flyways, but they fan out to the Atlantic coast and are not uncommon in Massachusetts from late September and October, where they feed on wild celery and eel grass, poached from Canvasbacks and Redheads. A few winter in that state.

[2] Courtesy Illinois Natural History Survey.

Baldpate

BLACK DUCK

(Anas rubripes)

FEMALE   MALE

COMMON NAMES

Black Mallard, Black, Blackie.

DESCRIPTION

A large, surface-feeding duck. Highly esteemed for sport and table, especially east of the Mississippi, where it is the most abundant of all waterfowl.

Adult male and female in flight. Large size, dark head and body, with sharply contrasting *white wing linings*. Upper surface all dusky with purplish wing patch (speculum), barred fore and aft with black. *The trailing edge of the wing patch is margined with white,* which is readily seen at close range with the naked eye and at long range with the aid of binoculars. Flight is swift. Keeps well up out of gunshot range. Does not readily decoy. Flies in small flocks on migration—often in "vee" formation or in line. A powerful beat of the wings, which slap the water, lifts it vertically into the air, reveal-ing bright red legs and feet in *adult males,* paler in *adult females.* The bill of the *adult male* is yellow in breeding (winter) plumage, chang-ing to greenish during the post-nuptial (eclipse) molt. *The adult female's* bill is yellowish, dusky-mottled. *Juvenile males* in first winter plumage have greenish, dusky-mottled bills and pinkish-brown legs and feet. *Juvenile females* have greenish, dusky-mottled bills and pinkish feet.

Adult male and female. Large size, general dusky hue, paler on the head and neck. *One white margin to trailing edge* of black-barred, purplish wing patch. Rides buoyantly; swims rapidly.

DISTRIBUTION

Breeding range from North Carolina west to Indiana and Min-nesota; north to the northern parts of Manitoba, Ontario, Quebec and Labrador. Casual in Saskatchewan and Alberta. Winters from the Great Lakes to the New England states, south to the Gulf coast states. *(See map.)*

NORTHWARD MIGRATION

Returns to the southerly portions of its breeding range in the latter part of March in small flocks composed of paired birds. Carries on to the more northerly portions in easy stages as the snow disappears, reaching its northerly limits late in May.

COURTSHIP AND NESTING

Pairing takes place on the wintering grounds in January and February. Courtship consists of the usual head-bobbing, much chasing of the female on the water and in the air. The female is almost invariably in the lead with one or more males following her every turn, dip or zoom; crowding her so closely as to batter wings. The male has a weak, wheezy quack—the female a loud, resounding quack which can be heard from afar.

FOOD

Mostly vegetable matter; pondweeds, grasses, sedges, smartweeds, and such grains as barley, wheat, buckwheat and corn, which they go for in a big way in the fall. Total vegetable matter is about 76 per cent on the coastal marshes, the balance being animal matter —mollusks and crustaceans. Birds in the interior have a larger vegetable diet, about 84 per cent. In the south they turn to rice, acorns, beechnuts and even huckleberries.

WEIGHTS

Male—*Average*: about 2 pounds, 12 ounces.
Female—*Average*: about 2 pounds, 8 ounces.

SOUTHWARD MIGRATION

The southern movement starts early in September and consists chiefly of juveniles. Seldom seen in large flocks. The flight increases

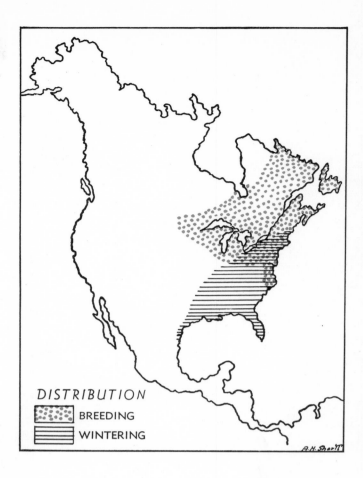

DISTRIBUTION
BREEDING
WINTERING

gradually as the season advances and reaches its peak as winter closes in. As the inland ponds freeze the ducks repair to the seacoasts and spend the day well out from shore in calm weather, or in the sheltered bays in rough. They return to the mud flats and marshes in the evening to feed.

The favorite sporting duck—excepting the Canvasback—of eastern wildfowlers.

Black Duck

BUFFLEHEAD

(*Glaucionetta albeola*[1])

MALE   FEMALE

COMMON NAMES

Butterball, Spirit Duck.

DESCRIPTION

A small black and white diving duck.

Adult male in flight. Small size; black and white markings; large head, short neck, chunky body; rapid wing beats. A broad white patch occupies the mid-section of the wing. A prominent triangular white patch separates the dark feathers of the forehead and hindhead. The dark head feathers are lustrous, with purple, green and violet sheens. Lower neck and underparts are white, back black with a few narrow white feather tips.

Adult male on water. Small size and dominant white appearance contrasting with black back. Relatively large head conspicu-

ously splashed with white makes identification easy. Bill blue-gray; feet flesh-colored.

Adult female in flight. Small size; generally drab appearance, with *small whitish patch below and behind the eye* and white wing patch (speculum) confined to seven inner secondaries. Rapid wing beats; short neck and large head.

Adult female on water. Small size; relatively large head with whitish patch below and behind eye. Otherwise dark brown appearance, darker on back and head. A drab little duck relieved only by the white head spot. Bill bluish-gray; feet dark gray.

NORTHWARD MIGRATION

Arrives in southern Canada about mid-April, except on the Pacific coast, where it is resident during the winter from southern Alaska south. Known only as a transient on the southern Canada prairies as it passes north to breed in the northern forested zone.

---

[1] The Genus *Charitonetta* is now united with *Glaucionetta*. See 20th Supplement to "The A.O.U. Check-list of North American Birds," *The Auk*, Volume 62 (1945), page 439.

COURTSHIP AND NESTING

Bent's description of the courtship during late April or early May is excellent: "The males are quite quarrelsome at this season and fight viciously among themselves for the possession of the females. The male is certainly a handsome creature as he swims in and out among the somber females, his bill pointing upwards, his neck extended and his beautiful head puffed out to twice its natural size and glistening in the sunlight. Standing erect, he struts about, as if supported by his feet and tail, with his bill drawn in upon his swelling bosom—a picture of pride and vanity, which is doubtless appreciated by his would-be mate. Suddenly he dives beneath her and, coming up immediately, deserts her and flies over to another female to repeat the process.

"He seems fickle or flirtatious in thus dividing his attentions, but perhaps he has not been graciously received or has been rebuffed. Sometimes he becomes coy and swims away until she shows interest enough to follow him. Eventually he finds the one best suited to him and the conjugal pact is sealed."

Apparently yearling females do not breed. Munro, in his study of the species, records that "large numbers of second-year females associate in flocks on the breeding grounds at the time when breeding females are incubating or caring for young."

Buffleheads nest in holes in trees—rarely in holes in cut banks. Old woodpecker cavities are used and may be any height above ground or water up to forty feet or so. Six to fourteen eggs are laid (usually ten or twelve) varying in color from ivory-yellow to pale olive-buff. They average 1.91 by 1.37 inches in size. The young fall from the nest to ground or water after the manner of young Goldeneyes or Wood Ducks.

FOOD

About 80 per cent of the food is animal matter, insects, crustaceans and mollusks being the chief items. Pondweeds and other aquatic vegetation make up the balance. The Bufflehead's food habits are not conducive to well-flavored flesh, consequently it is not regarded as a good table bird and is not hunted to any great extent.

WEIGHTS

Male—*Average of 17:* 1 pound. *Extremes:* 13 ounces to 1 pound, 4 ounces.

Female—*Average of 14:* 12 ounces. *Extremes:* 8 ounces to 1 pound 5 ounces.

SOUTHWARD MIGRATION

The hardy little Bufflehead is a late migrant, appearing in small flocks in October and never more than locally on the prairies. The

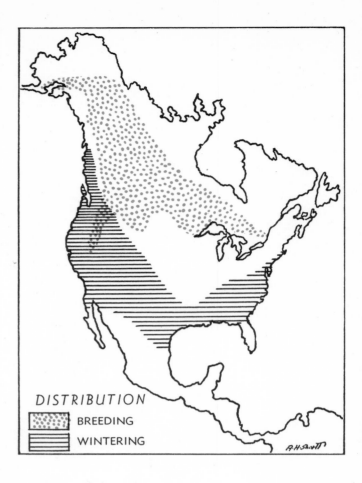

DISTRIBUTION
- ⣿ BREEDING
- ≡ WINTERING

height of the migration is in the first few days of November—just before freeze-up—and the principal line of flight in Manitoba is through the evergreen forest region in the eastern part of the province.

DISTRIBUTION

Found only in North America. "Breeds from British Columbia, southern Yukon territory, west-central Alaska, northern Mackenzie, Great Slave Lake and southwestern coats of Hudson and James Bays to northern Montana; reported as breeding formerly in Maine, New Brunswick, Wisconsin, Iowa and Wyoming, and recently at lakes in northeastern California. Winters from the Aleutians and Commander Islands and the Alaska peninsula south to central Mexico and Lower California, and from northwestern Montana, Great Lakes and the coast of Maine to South Carolina, northern Florida and the Gulf coasts of Louisiana and Texas. Casual in Greenland, Bermuda, Cuba, Puerto Rico and the Hawaiian Islands.

REFERENCES

Hochbaum, H. Albert, *The Canvasback on a Prairie Marsh*, 1944.
Kortright, Francis H., *The Ducks, Geese and Swans of North America*, 1942.
Munro, J. A., "Studies of Waterfowl in British Columbia: Buffleheads," *Canadian Journal of Research*, 1942.
The A.O.U. Check-list of North American Birds (Fourth Edition), 1931.

Bufflehead

CANVASBACK

(Aythya valisineria)

MALE   FEMALE

COMMON NAME

Can.

DESCRIPTION

A large diving duck with long, wedge-shaped head. Highly regarded for sport and table.

Adult male in flight. Large size; long head and neck appear dark; black breast; white underbody; dark tail. On migration this species often flies in perfect "vee" formation, their long, pointed wings carrying them forward with great speed—estimated up to 55 miles per hour.

Adult male on water. Large, white-backed bird with long, wedge-shaped head. The head and neck are reddish-chestnut—clearly seen in good light—darker on crown and throat. Sets low in water and dives almost as quickly and neatly as a loon.

Adult female in flight. Large size and distinctive shape of head are best field marks. Generally darker than male and devoid of contrasting colors. Overall effect brownish, paler on underparts.

Adult female on water. Large brownish bird with yellowish-brown head and neck. The large, wedge-shaped head lacking any brow contour avoids confusion with similarly colored female Redhead.

NORTHWARD MIGRATION

Canvasbacks fly north well behind the retreating snowline. They pass through Pennsylvania, Wisconsin and Minnesota usually during the last half of March and first ten days of April. Arrives in southern prairie provinces of Canada about third week in April—a few days earlier in early seasons. First arrivals are paired birds, in small companies; later migrants largely unpaired.

COURTSHIP AND NESTING

Hochbaum's study of the Canvasback on the Delta Marshes in Manitoba is our best source of information on the courtship and nesting of this prime favorite of the sportsman. The courting males indulge in curious antics. The head is thrown back until it touches the back. In another posture the male stretches his neck to the utmost and swims around the female and other suitors like a strutting martinet. Another stunt, "the sneak," consists of stretching the head and neck out flat along the water. When rival males threaten each other, they crouch with the neck drawn in and head thrust forward. Rough-and-tumble tussles may follow, but no serious damage is done. The displaying males crowd the female, but she drives them away until, finally, one secures a privileged position on her flank. This, apparently, constitutes pairing.

In nuptial flight the drake follows the female and tries to catch her tail feathers in his bill. "Now and again he succeeds, literally 'cracking the whip' behind as she attempts to free herself." Copulation takes place in the water.

The nest is a bulky, well-made structure among hardstem bulrush, cattail, cane reeds (*Phragmites*) growing in shallow water; occasionally in meadowgrass or base of willow on dry land close to water. Nesting starts in last few days of April and early in May. Incubation period 24 to 28 days. The nest is made of materials in which it is concealed, lined with gray down. Six to thirteen grayish-olive or greenish-drab eggs, averaging 2.75 by 1.72, inches are laid. The nests frequently have Redhead, Ruddy or Lesser Scaup's eggs added, the Redhead being the more frequent offender.

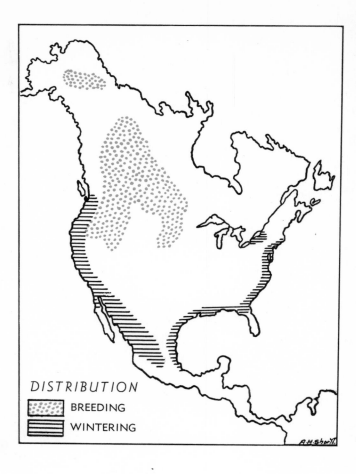

DISTRIBUTION
- [dotted] BREEDING
- [hatched] WINTERING

FOOD

Food consists of 80 per cent vegetable matter, the chief items being pondweeds, wild celery, duck potato, grasses (including foxtail and wild rice), sedges, water lily, burr-reeds, water milfoil and muskgrass (*Chara*). The balance—20 per cent animal matter— mollusks, insects, small fish. Wild celery (*Vallisneria spiralis*)—a favorite food in the eastern States—is said to impart a delicious flavor to its flesh.

WEIGHTS

Male—*Average of 102:* 3 pounds. *Extremes:* 2 pounds, 4 ounces to 3 pounds, 9 ounces.

Female—*Average of 102:* 2 pounds, 13 ounces. *Extremes:* 1 pound, 14 ounces to 3 pounds, 6 ounces.

SOUTHWARD MIGRATION

Aerial surveys of northern lakes in August revealed thousands of flightless drakes, which evidently gather from great distances to molt. They return to the southern marshes late in September and

leave for their wintering grounds between October 14 and 24. Few Canvasbacks are seen after the mass exodus takes place. The migration is made up of small groups.

DISTRIBUTION

Breeds from Alaska (Fort Yukon) and Great Slave Lake to central Manitoba, central-western Nebraska, northern New Mexico, northern Utah, and western Nevada, occasionally east to southern Minnesota and southern Wisconsin. Winters from southern British Columbia south along the Pacific coast to Mexico, and from northwestern Montana, northern Colorado, northeastern Arkansas, southern Illinois, and Chesapeake Bay south to Florida, the Gulf coast of Louisiana, Texas, central Mexico and, rarely, Guatemala. Casual or accidental in Bermuda, New Brunswick and Nova Scotia.

REFERENCES

Hochbaum, H. Albert, *The Canvasback on a Prairie Marsh*, 1944.
Kortright, Francis H., *The Ducks, Geese and Swans of North America*, 1942.
Roberts, Thomas S., *Birds of Minnesota*, 1932.
The A.O.U. Check-list of North American Birds (Fourth Edition), 1931.
——— (20th Supplement), *The Auk*, Volume 62, Number 3 (July, 1945), page 438.

Canvasback

AMERICAN EIDER

(Somateria mollissima dresseri)

FEMALE   MALE

COMMON NAME

Sea Duck.

DESCRIPTION

Large, black and white duck (male) with heavy wedge-shaped head. Female is rich brown streaked with black. The American Eider is a subspecies of the Common Eider (*S.m. mollissima*) of Europe. Other subspecies in America are Northern Eider (*S.m. borealis*), Pacific Eider (*S.m. v-nigra*) and Hudson Bay Eider (*S.m. sedentaria*). They differ from each other in such details as color, size and shape of bill and bill processes, extent of greenish head-patches, and, in the Pacific Eider, the consistent presence of a black "vee"-shaped mark under the chin. Otherwise the general coloration and pattern is similar for all.

Adult male in flight. Large size; large, low-hung head; thick neck. Black breast, belly and tail; black and white wings; white back, chest, neck and head. Black crown patch. Flat profile of bill and head gives a wedge-shaped appearance like that of the Canvasback. Fly close to water in heavy, labored flight, although speedy.

Adult male on water. Large size. White back and foreparts and black sides.

Adult female in flight. Large size. Uniform dark plumage. Head showing straight-line profile.

Adult female on water. Large size. Uniform rich-brown plumage heavily barred with black. Large head and straight-line profile. Swims with bill usually pointed down and neck drawn in.

DISTRIBUTION AND MIGRATION

The American Eider breeds on the coastal islands of Labrador south of Hamilton Inlet, Newfoundland, eastern Quebec, Nova Scotia, and Maine; also on Hudson Bay and James Bay as far north as Southampton Island and Cape Fullerton. Recently the Hudson Bay Eider has been accorded subspecific status and is considered a resident on Hudson Bay from Cape Fullerton south into James Bay.

The Northern Eider breeds on the coastal islands of Greenland and the eastern Arctic islands, south on the Atlantic coast to Labrador (Hamilton Inlet) and Quebec. They winter from southern Greenland to the coast of Maine, rarely to Massachusetts and Connecticut. In parts of the winter range they are found in company with the American Eider, which winters on the seacoast from Newfoundland and the Gulf of St. Lawrence to Massachusetts and rarely to Virginia. They also interbreed. The Pacific Eider breeds on the Siberian and Arctic coasts from Alaska to Coronation Gulf and on Banks and Victoria Islands; south on both coasts of the Bering Sea to the Commander and Aleutian Islands; and east along the south side of the Alaskan peninsula to Kodiac Island and Cook Inlet. Winters mainly in the vicinity of the Aleutian Islands and Alaska peninsula, moving but little south of its breeding range.

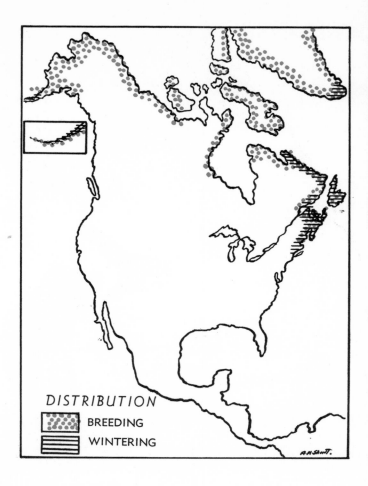

DISTRIBUTION

- (dotted) BREEDING
- (hatched) WINTERING

COURTSHIP AND NESTING

Courtship and nesting is similar for all races, and display is said not to be elaborate. "Drakes swim with head held high and neck stiff, uttering crooning call with upward jerk of the bill. Most complete performance is when head is drawn rigidly down, bill resting on breast, head then raised until it points vertically upwards, when it may or may not be opened to emit display note." Often drakes rise up in water, in Mallard-like fashion, to display their black underparts; but movement may be continued in upthrow of bill as note is uttered, with downward jerk at end.

"The nests are placed on the ground and generally close to salt water, though often nests are found a hundred yards or more from water. The nesting site may be open to the sky in a depression among the rocks of a barren island, but it is often partially or wholly concealed among and under spruce, alder or laurel bushes or in the grass or rushes. The nest itself is made of seaweeds, mosses, sticks, leaves and grasses matted together, but is chiefly distinguished for the famous eider down, which is plucked by the mother from her breast. The down is of a dull gray color, very soft, light, warm, and usually supplied in such liberal amounts that the eggs can be completely covered when the sitting bird is absent.

"The eggs are oval in shape, of a lusterless exterior, as if the lime had been put on with a coarse brush. The color is olive green, varying in depth, and sometimes tinged with brownish. Four eggs constitute the usual setting, which, however, varies from three to six eggs, the average size of which is 2.99 by 2 inches. These are the largest of ducks' eggs. The period of incubation is 28 days and is performed by the female alone." (Kortright)

FOOD

Food consists almost entirely of animal matter (96 per cent), which includes mollusks (chiefly blue mussel), crustaceans, echinoderms (including sea urchins) and insects. A little more plant food is taken during summer.

WEIGHTS

Male—*Average of 3:* 4 pounds, 6 ounces. *Extremes:* 3 pounds, 15 ounces to 4 pounds, 10 ounces.

Female—*Average of 8:* 3 pounds, 6 ounces. *Extremes:* 2 pounds, 10 ounces to 3 pounds, 12 ounces.

REFERENCES

Kortright, Francis H., *The Ducks, Geese and Swans of North America*, 1942.
Witherby, Jourdain, Ticehurst and Tucker, *Handbook of British Birds* (Volume 3), 1943.
The A.O.U. Check-list of North American Birds (Fourth Edition), 1931.
——— (Supplement), *The Auk*, July, 1944.
——— (Supplement), *The Auk*, July, 1946.

American Eider

KING EIDER

(S. spectabilis)

MALE   FEMALE

COMMON NAME

King-a-lik (Eskimo).

DESCRIPTION

A large, heavy-bodied sea duck. The male is a strikingly beautiful bird with a bizarre pattern and color combination unlike that of any other species. The female is a rich brown, heavily barred duck without conspicuous markings.

Adult male in flight. Male distinguished from other eiders by *black back and remarkable shape and coloring of head and bill. The bill "is orange with broad shield at base expanding to form a huge and conspicuous knob* in breeding season, rising up to level of top of crown and bordered by black feathers. Crown and nape pale blue-gray; sides of face white-tinged pale green; black streak on either side of throat, meeting in a 'vee' in front." Upper breast creamy-white; rest of underparts black. Large white patches on forewings and white spot on flank at base of tail.

Adult male on water. Large size. In winter plumage, the creamy-white foreparts, black hindparts and curiously shaped orange bill and frontal shield, separated from the blue-gray crown and nape by black, make identification easy.

Adult female in flight. Large size. Uniform rusty or buffy brown. Lighter on throat. Heavily barred with darker brown. Difficult to distinguish from other large eider females.

Adult female on water. Large size. Brown, heavily barred with darker brown. Best identified by association with her consort.

DISTRIBUTION

Circumpolar. Breeds from both coasts of Greenland and entire Arctic coast of Canada and Alaska south to Hudson Strait, northern Labrador, northern Hudson Bay and James Bay. On the Pacific side, St. Lawrence and St. Matthew Islands, and Bering Sea; also on the Arctic coast of Siberia, Novaya Zemlya, and Spitzbergen. Winters from southern Greenland to the coast of Massachusetts and New York, more rarely to Virginia and the Great Lakes, occasionally farther in the interior, and from Bering Sea to the Aleutians, Kodiak and Shumagin Islands; also Iceland, Faroes, Great Britain (rare), Norway, Denmark, Holland, northern Russia and Finland. Casual in Italy, France, Hungary and southern Russia.

NORTHWARD MIGRATION

More common in the northern Pacific area. Brandt, referring to the migration at Hooper Bay, Alaska, states, "The King Eider greatly overshadows in numbers any species found there. It flew over Point Dall in such teeming multitudes that its migration was the most conspicuous feature. . . . In a few hours on a few days an estimate of 125,000 was made between May 4–19. The flight was often heaviest during the night, and especially towards the early morning, when no record was kept. . . . Their far-flung legions on thunderous pinions all push on to the Alaskan north; . . . and their transmarine passage, wondrous to witness, forms one of the grandest bird flights on the North American continent."

COURTSHIP AND NESTING

Courtship display is not elaborate. Head-bobbing indicates sexually active birds of both sexes. "Most complete display by male is when head is drawn rigidly down, bill resting on breast, head then raised until it points vertically upwards, when it may or may not be opened to emit display note. Often drakes rise up in water in Mallard-like fashion, but movement may be continued in upthrow of bill as note is uttered with downward jerk at end."

Shows a preference to nest on tundra in or near freshwater ponds. Though a good many pairs may nest in a district, the nests are widely scattered and often far apart (Witherby, et al.). Nest is mostly made of sooty-brown down with a few heather stems and grasses. Concealment seems to be a matter of indifference. The eggs, usually four to seven, are variable shades of olive-buff and measure 2.66 by 1.76 inches. The young do not mature the following spring and perhaps not during their second, according to Bent.

FOOD

Almost exclusively animal matter (95 per cent), of which mollusks and crustaceans are predominant. Eel grass, algae and miscella-

DISTRIBUTION
BREEDING
WINTERING

neous items make up the small percentage of vegetable matter in 85 specimens collected in Alaska, Canada, United States and Siberia.

WEIGHTS

Male—*Average of 13:* 4 pounds. *Extremes:* 3 pounds, 11 ounces to 4 pounds, 7 ounces.
Female—*Average of 8:* 3 pounds, 10 ounces. *Extremes:* 2 pounds, 12 ounces to 4 pounds, 2 ounces.

REFERENCES

Brandt, Herbert, *Alaska Bird Trails,* 1943.
Kortright, Francis H., *The Ducks, Geese and Swans of North America,* 1942.
Witherby, Jourdain, Ticehurst and Tucker, *Handbook of British Birds,* 1943.
The A.O.U. Check-list of North American Birds (Fourth Edition), 1931.

King Eider

SPECTACLED EIDER

(Arctonetta fischeri)

MALE   FEMALE

COMMON NAMES

Fischer's Eider, Kow-uk (Eskimo).

DESCRIPTION

A medium-sized eider. The male is distinguished by a white patch rimmed with black around eye, giving the appearance of spectacles. The female is cinnamon brown with feather edges of black. A paler patch around eye suggests the spectacles of the male.

Adult male in flight. Smaller than Pacific Eider, larger than Steller's. Similar heavy-bodied appearance in flight. Entirely black underparts except throat and neck. White foreback and patches on mid-forewing. Otherwise, wings and lower back and tail are black or dark brown. Head is pale green with *conspicuous white patch around eye, which is bordered with black to create the illusion of spectacles.* This feature can be seen at a considerable distance.

Adult male on water. A large sea duck with black sides and tail, white back and throat, yellow bill and pale green head, with prominent white patch around eye bordered with black.

Adult female in flight. A dark, almost black duck without conspicuous markings. Indistinguishable from other female eiders except by association with her mate.

Adult female on water. A cinnamon-brown eider with heavy black bars on brown feathers. A paler patch around eye—suggesting the spectacles—can be seen at close range.

DISTRIBUTION

Breeds on the Arctic coasts of Siberia and Alaska from the Lena River to Point Barrow (occasionally to Colville River) south, on the Bering Sea coast of Alaska, to the mouth of the Kuskoquim River. Winters in the vicinity of the Aleutian and Pribilof Islands, and rarely eastward along the south side of the Alaskan peninsula to Sanak Island.

NORTHWARD MIGRATION

This least common and most range-restricted species of eider migrates in May and June on the Alaskan side of the Bering Sea. The migration is long and drawn out, for Brandt records the first migrants on May 5 and the peak about May 22 in the Hooper Bay region. Farther north at Cape Prince of Wales, Bailey noted the first migrants on May 16, together with many flights on June 3 and more on June 23.

COURTSHIP AND NESTING

Brandt states, "The real glory of the male, however, is his brilliant headdress of satiny light olive-green and his conspicuous white spectacles rimmed with black. . . . The silky, hair-like feathers on the back of his crown normally hang down; and, when he is amorously displaying his charms to lady love, they stand erect as a hairy crest. As he floats on the reflecting surface of a calm tundra pond, his crest opening and closing like a fan, and his white scapulars erected over his back, he is indeed worthy of the loving adoration of his gentle sweetheart.

"The Spectacled Eider chooses its nesting site on the grassy flats in the immediate vicinity of water, often selecting an island in a small pond. Here, in unobstructed view of the ground, a slight depression is made by the female in the soft turf and scantily lined with grass stems. Then, like all the rest of the ducks breeding in that region, she plucks from her breast a quantity of soft fluffy down, amidst which her large olive eggs find a cozy cradle."

The eggs, which become nest stained to a buffy hue as incubation proceeds, are usually five or six, although as many as nine have been recorded. They measure 2.57 by 1.76 inches.

FOOD

Little is known of the feeding habits, but studies of the limited numbers of stomachs analyzed disclose that about 75 per cent of the food is animal matter. Mollusks, insects and crustaceans are the most prominent items. Pondweeds, crowberry, marestail and sedges form items in the vegetable diet.

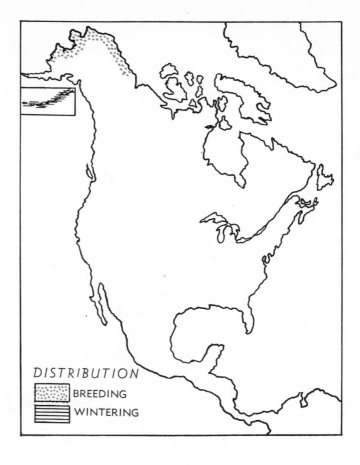

DISTRIBUTION

BREEDING

WINTERING

WEIGHTS

Male—*Average of 8:* 3 pounds, 10 ounces. *Extremes:* 3 pounds, 3 ounces to 3 pounds, 12 ounces.

Female—*Average of 4:* 3 pounds, 10 ounces. *Extremes:* 3 pounds, 6 ounces to 3 pounds, 14 ounces.

REFERENCES

Bailey, Alfred M., *The Birds of Cape Prince of Wales, Alaska,* 1943.
Brandt, Herbert, *Alaska Bird Trails,* 1943.
Kortright, Francis H., *The Ducks, Geese and Swans of North America,* 1942.
The A.O.U. Check-list of North American Birds (Fourth Edition), 1931.

Spectacled Eider

STELLER'S EIDER

(Polysticta stelleri)

MALE   FEMALE

COMMON NAME

A-noch-a-nee-sak-kuk (Eskimo).

DESCRIPTION

Smallest, speediest and most beautiful of the eiders. Steller's Eider was named in 1769 by the Russian ornithologist Pallas in honor of the German naturalist George Wilhelm Steller (1709–1746), who accompanied Bering on his voyage to the sea bearing his name, during which the species was discovered.

Adult male in flight. Small size; neat, trim outline (as compared with the other heavy-bodied eiders); black and white pattern; white head, dark patch on nape; chestnut-buff breast and belly, shading to paler on flanks. Wings whistle like Goldeneyes in flight.

Adult male on water. "Hind part of body and wings black with crescent-shaped white mark on wings; throat, collar and center of back also black. The long scapulars which curve over the white forewing are banded lengthwise with black and white." The bill is grayish-blue and more duck-like than the bill of the other eiders. Head white with tufts of greenish feathers behind crown and in front of eye. Eye is encircled by black.

Adult female in flight. Small size; trim outline; dark brown head and body; upper side of wings dark with *purplish-blue wing patch bordered fore and aft with white* like the Mallard. Wing linings white.

Adult female on water. Dark brown body with Mallard-like speculum.

NORTHWARD MIGRATION

Brandt records that Steller's Eider is the last of the sea ducks to migrate over Hooper Bay, Alaska (from its wintering grounds around the Aleutian Islands). It was first recorded on May 18 and continued to pass in limited numbers for ten days. Two years later (1922) Bailey records the first arrivals at Cape Prince of Wales on May 12. The main migration was observed on May 29. This is farther north than Hooper Bay.

In migration they sometimes fly close to the ground at great speed and follow every contour of the land in a long wavy line after the manner of eiders and scoters. Brandt says non-breeding yearlings appear to stay south of the breeding range, since only three in immature plumage were seen among the migrants.

COURTSHIP AND NESTING

"A characteristic feature of courtship is manner in which tawny breast of male is displayed, the bird rising half out of water as he follows female (*H.M.S. Blair*)."—*Handbook of British Birds*.

Brandt says, "By May 25 we often saw small flocks of mated pairs of the Steller's Eider inland on the ice-margined ponds, where they seemed very gentle and undemonstrative. They often gathered on the shore of a tidewater pond, where the handsome males exhibited their beautiful shining colors to the demure females. As late as June 9 small flocks were flying about from pond to pond, although migration had apparently ceased. They were frequently seen feeding along the margins of shallow pools, tipping up like Mallards, their tails pointing to the zenith. Not only was the Steller's Eider the last of the eiders to reach its breeding grounds about Hooper Bay, but it was also the latest to nest, for on June 18 all the eggs observed were perfectly fresh.

"We found the Steller's Eider of common occurrence on the tidewater flats, where it selects for its nesting site a small eminence near a body of water. There it often builds up a substantial nest of grass, which it lines warmly with the almost black down which the female plucks from her breast. Shortly after the middle of June she lays the full complement of six to nine eggs." The eggs are olive-buff when fresh or cleaned—saccardo-umber when nest stained. Average measurement of forty eggs: 2.31 by 1.61 inches.

FOOD

Over 80 per cent animal matter: crustaceans, mollusks, insects, annelid worms, sand dollars, fishes, in that order of preference. Pondweeds, crowberries and algae form the bulk of the small amount of vegetable matter.

WEIGHTS

Male—*Average of 5:* 1 pound, 15 ounces. *Extremes:* 1 pound, 14 ounces to 2 pounds, 2 ounces.

DISTRIBUTION
BREEDING
WINTERING

Female—*Average of 5:* 1 pound, 15 ounces. *Extremes:* 1 pound, 14 ounces to 2 pounds.

DISTRIBUTION

Breeds on the Arctic coasts of Siberia and Alaska. Winters on coasts of northern Scandinavia and northern Pacific (Aleutian and Commander Islands, Kuriles and southern Alaska). Accidental in England, Quebec, Greenland, France, Germany, Denmark and Japan.

REFERENCES

Bailey, Alfred M., *The Birds of Cape Prince of Wales, Alaska*, 1943.
Brandt, Herbert, *Alaska Bird Trails*, 1943.
Kortright, Francis H., *The Ducks, Geese and Swans of North America*, 1942.
Witherby, Jourdain, Ticehurst and Tucker, *Handbook of British Birds* (Volume 3), 1943.
The A.O.U. Check-list of North American Birds (Fourth Edition), 1931.

Steller's Eider

GADWALL

(Chaulelasmus streperus)

MALE   FEMALE

COMMON NAMES

Gray duck, Gadwell.

DESCRIPTION

A fairly large, surface-feeding duck. Has shown a gratifying increase in numbers during the last five years.

Adult male in flight. Fairly large size; generally gray appearance with a *conspicuous rectangular white patch on hind wing close to body.* The only North American duck with a white speculum (wing patch).

Adult male on water. Almost as large as Mallard. Gray duck with velvety black rear end. *White patch (rectangular) high up on side toward tail.*

Adult female in flight. Fairly large size; generally grayish appearance relieved only by the *white patches on wings close to body.* This field mark is unlike that of any other duck.

Adult female on water. Grayish duck with small, neat head; yellowish bill and feet. May be easily mistaken for female Mallard or female Pintail. White patch high up on side near tail not always visible and not so prominent as in male.

DISTRIBUTION

The most cosmopolitan of ducks. World-wide in distribution except in South America and Australia. Its breeding range in North America is chiefly on the great plains from the Mississippi west to California; north to southern British Columbia, central Alberta, central Saskatchewan, central Manitoba; east and north to Keewatin (Eskimo Point, Hudson Bay).

Winters from southern British Columbia, central and southern States south to Mexico.

Breeds also in Iceland, the British Isles, Europe, Asia and northern Africa. Winters deep into Africa, India, Burma and China.

NORTHWARD MIGRATION

The Gadwall moves northward well behind the retreating snow-line in March and April, arriving in southern Canada from the middle of April to early May. The peak of migration is about May 5.

COURTSHIP AND NESTING

"In June, a band of twelve or fourteen Gadwall drakes after one hen is not an uncommon sight," remarks Al Hochbaum in *The Canvasback on a Prairie Marsh*.[1] These wild courtship flights, in which one female leads one or many drakes a merry chase, are a feature of the marsh skyways in May and June. She seems to enjoy this pursuit by many males—the more the merrier—as much as any debutante at her coming-out party.

On the water, the antics of one or more males before a female are similar to those of other surface feeders. There is much head-bobbing, threats and maneuvering between rivals, plumage-displaying and love play. When the female finally makes her choice, she and her mate combine to drive off the disappointed suitors, who soon depart to try their luck elsewhere.

The nest is always on dry land at some distance from water. An island is a favored location, but hay meadows or the margins of willow swales are well patronized. The nest is deeply cupped and lined with grasses. The eggs are creamy-white, seven to fifteen in number (usually ten or twelve), well protected after incubation is under way with a warm blanket of down plucked from the female's own breast.[2] The eggs average 2.18 inches by 1.56 inches. Incubation period is said to be 28 days, but in the Delta Duck Hatchery, Ward found the period in the incubators to vary from 21 to 25 days— average 24 days.

FOOD

The Gadwall seems to dive for food more frequently than other surface-feeding ducks, although the young of all species dive quite readily. The Gadwall prefers to feed in the shallow marshes and sloughs where pondweeds, sedges, algae and other aquatic vegetation form more than 90 per cent of its intake. Young Gadwall, during the

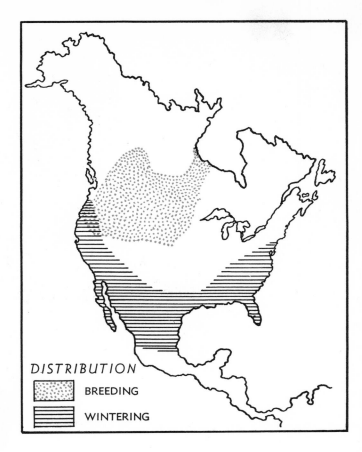

DISTRIBUTION

▨ BREEDING

▤ WINTERING

period of rapid growth, feed largely, if not exclusively, on aquatic and terrestrial insects and larvae.

WEIGHTS

Male—*Average of 122:* 2 pounds. *Extremes:* 1 pound, 9 ounces to 2 pounds, 8 ounces.

Female—*Average of 101:* 1 pound, 13 ounces. *Extremes:* 1 pound, 5 ounces to 2 pounds, 4 ounces.

SOUTHWARD MIGRATION

In normal fall weather conditions, Gadwall migrate from Canada during the first half of October. A few remain until freeze-up, which is usually about November 5. The migration is chiefly down the Central and Mississippi flyways, with important migration routes branching off to the Pacific and Atlantic coasts.

---

[1] For further details on territorial arrangements and behavior, we refer our readers to H. Albert Hochbaum's *The Canvasback on a Prairie Marsh*. This work, published in 1944 by the American Wildlife Institute, under whose auspices research was carried out at Delta, Manitoba, earned for its author the Brewster Award in Ornithology— the highest award of merit of the American Ornithologists Union.

[2] In a nesting study on Kazan Lake, northern Saskatchewan, by T. E. Randall for Ducks Unlimited in 1942, 117 Gadwall's nests containing 1,322 eggs were found. Clutches ranged from 7 to 15, averaged 11.3 per clutch.

Gadwall

AMERICAN GOLDENEYE

(Glaucionetta clangula americana)

FEMALE   MALE

COMMON NAMES

Whistler, Whistle-wing.

DESCRIPTION

A medium-sized diving duck.

Adult male in flight. Medium size; black and white pattern; short neck; big round, black head and loud, penetrating whistle of wings make identification easy. Shows more white than any other duck except the larger American Merganser. The white wing patch appears to occupy about half the wing area. Round white spot in front of and below eye can be seen under favorable conditions.

Adult male on water. Medium size; large amount of white with black head, back and rear end. Large, tufty head with white spot between bill and eye.

Adult female in flight. Medium size; brownish bird with white breast and whitish wing patch crossed by a dark bar.

Adult female on water. Appears smaller than male and rides lower in water. Brown head and white collar (incomplete behind) are readily seen.

Note: The female American Goldeneye cannot be distinguished with certainty in the field from the female Barrow's Goldeneye.

NORTHWARD MIGRATION

The Goldeneye is a hardy bird and winters wherever open water is found. Migrates in small parties. The first arrivals in southern Canada are usually seen in early April, and migration is general about the middle of the month.

COURTSHIP AND NESTING

Courtship is as elaborate and "full of life" as in any other species. The males swim around a female with head and cheek feathers "puffed out" and glinting with lustrous purple and green.

37

They throw up the bill, utter a harsh cry and snap the head back until it touches the rump. The head is jerked back to normal and, at the same time, the bird plunges forward and kicks water out behind, displaying his breast, wings and orange-colored feet. One after the other (or together), the males go through this performance, which makes an animated and noisy scene indeed.

Goldeneyes nest in holes in trees, in cottage chimneys and in artificial nest boxes. Tree nesting is their natural habit. Five to nineteen olive-green eggs are laid in the cavity, which may be from two to fifteen feet below the entrance hole. The eggs measure 2.35 by 1.71 inches. Incubation period about 21 days. Large clutches are frequent but ten or twelve eggs are average.

At the call of the female, the young tumble out of the hole like peas popping out of a pod. They seem to take no harm from falls of twenty feet or more onto land or into water. The nesting range is chiefly in areas where northern pike (*Esox lucius*) infest the waters. The young quite often climb on the female's back for transportation over dangerous open stretches. Otherwise they swim in a compact bunch behind the female—touching each other—and changing direction as one bird. Presumably this consolidation presents a large, solid body to the lurking "jackfish" below, and attack is avoided.

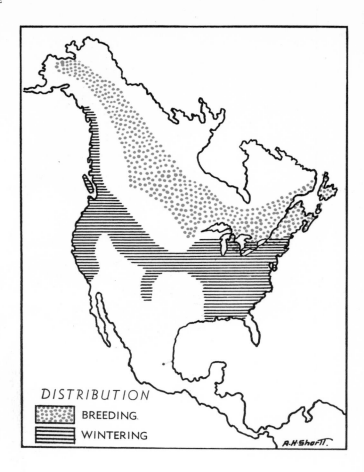

DISTRIBUTION
░ BREEDING
▬ WINTERING

FOOD

About three quarters of the diet is animal matter, which probably accounts for its second rating as a table bird. Crustaceans: 32.42 per cent; aquatic insects: 27.98 per cent; mollusks: 9.71 per cent; fishes: 3.16 per cent. Plant food, 26.09 per cent, is chiefly pondweeds, wild celery, spatterdocks and bulrush.

WEIGHTS

Male—*Average of 36:* 2 pounds, 2½ ounces. *Extremes:* 1 pound, 9 ounces to 2½ pounds, 14 ounces.

Female—*Average of 33:* 1 pound, 11½ ounces. *Extremes:* 1 pound, 6 ounces to 2 pounds, 4 ounces.

SOUTHWARD MIGRATION

Goldeneyes are never seen in large flocks. They appear in small parties and swoop in with a verve, speed and whistle that bring a thrill to the most experienced gunner. They pop up out of nowhere in October and November in Canada—on their way south—and are as wary or trusting as previous experience with mankind dictates. They are not considered good game and the discriminating hunters

pass them up for more desirable table birds. They can, however, put enough "gimp" into a dull day to please the most blasé gunner, especially on the foulest, coldest, most uncomfortable day in late fall.

DISTRIBUTION

The American Goldeneye is a subspecies of the Goldeneye of Europe and Asia. It breeds from Newfoundland to Alaska wherever suitable nesting sites can be found in the forested regions. It winters from the Aleutians, the southern Canadian provinces and Maine, south, wherever open water is found, to southern California, Arkansas and the states east of the Mississippi to the Gulf coast.

REFERENCES

Cottam, Clarence, "Food Habits of North American Diving Ducks," *U.S. Department of Agriculture Technical Bulletin 643*, 1939.

Coward, T. A., *Birds of Wayside and Woodland*, 1936.

Hochbaum, H. Albert, *The Canvasback on a Prairie Marsh*, 1944.

Kortright, Francis H., *The Ducks, Geese and Swans of North America*, 1942.

The A.O.U. Check-list of North American Birds (Fourth Edition), 1931.

American Goldeneye

BARROW'S GOLDENEYE

(G. islandica)

MALE   FEMALE

COMMON NAME

Whistler.

DESCRIPTION

A medium-sized diving duck.

Adult male in flight. Medium size; black and white pattern; short neck; large, tufty head. Separated from the adult male American Goldeneye by the much larger amount of black on the sides.

Adult male on water. Medium size; large, tufty, black head with *purplish sheen and white, crescent-shaped spot in front of eye.* Head feathers, semi-crested, point backwards. Shows more black on back and sides than the American Goldeneye.

Adult female in flight. Medium size; brownish-gray above; white breast. Indistinguishable from female American Goldeneye or from juveniles of both sexes.

Adult female on water. Similar to female American Goldeneye and cannot be separated in life with any degree of certainty.

DISTRIBUTION

Breeds in southern Greenland, Iceland and on the Labrador coast; also from southern Alaska, British Columbia, western Alberta south to California (Sierra Nevada) and southern Colorado. Winters on the Atlantic coast from the Gulf of St. Lawrence to Maine (rarely farther) and on the Pacific coast from southern Alaska to central California.

NORTHWARD MIGRATION

There are two distinct, widely separated groups of Barrow's Goldeneyes, one in the Atlantic and one in the Pacific, the latter being numerically superior. The Atlantic group migrates north from Maine and the Gulf of St. Lawrence in March as soon as weather permits. The Pacific group moves from the coastal waters to interior lakes and streams in March and April, ascending in altitude up to 10,000 feet as the spring break-up progresses. The northward migration extends over a period of about six weeks.

41

COURTSHIP AND NESTING

Munro (1939) states, "The courtship period is of long duration, commencing on the coast and reaching its greatest activity in April on the lakes of the interior (British Columbia), where large concentrations take place." The display by the male includes the "head throw," the "neck stretch," head-bobbing and "threat" posture, in which he may surge over the water toward a female or rival male. One or several males will chase a female in rapid flights around the lake or through or above the trees.

The nest is usually in tree cavities (rarely in burrows of the yellow-footed marmot) in British Columbia; in holes in stream banks or among rocks, or even on the ground under bushes, in Iceland and southern Greenland. The tree nests may be up to fifty feet above ground; lower down, they may be found in stubs standing in water or back in the woods a mile or more away. Eight to twelve, sometimes more, olive-green eggs, measuring 2.41 by 1.73 inches, are laid. The young reach the ground by tumbling from the nest at the call of the female, as is true with the Wood Duck and American Goldeneye. *Goldeneyes (both species) do not breed until their second year.*

FOOD

Animal matter constitutes more than 75 per cent of the diet: salmon eggs and flesh, crustaceans, aquatic insects, larvae and mollusks. Munro's analysis of food taken by specimens collected in the interior of British Columbia revealed 96 per cent animal matter. Vegetable matter is but a small part of its diet, and its reputation as a table bird is low.

WEIGHTS

Very little information is available on the weights of Barrow's Goldeneye. Kortright (1942) lists the weight of only one specimen of each sex:

Male—2 pounds, 14 ounces.
Female—1 pound, 10 ounces.

SOUTHWARD MIGRATION

Adult and yearling males leave the incubating females on the breeding grounds about the beginning of June, and very few are

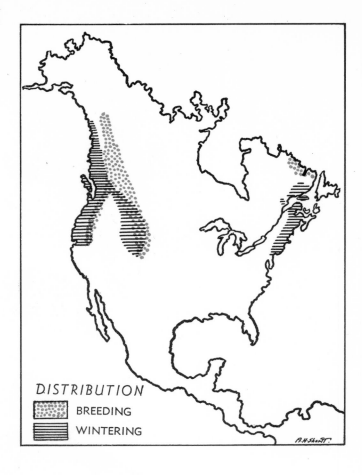

DISTRIBUTION
BREEDING
WINTERING

seen beyond the middle of the month. They apparently gather on the coasts and, perhaps, some interior lakes. In July and August the interior populations are made up of adult females with young and yearling females. During August–September adult and yearling females molt and migrate. In September–October young of the year migrate. November and December finds the total population associating on coastal waters. On the Atlantic coast the species appears on the wintering grounds late in October.

REFERENCES

Kortright, Francis H., *The Ducks, Geese and Swans of North America*, 1942.
Munro, J. A., trans., Royal Canadian Institute, "Studies of Waterfowl in British Columbia: Barrow's Goldeneye, American Goldeneye," October, 1939.
The A.O.U. Check-list of North American Birds (Fourth Edition), 1931.

Barrow's Goldeneye

HARLEQUIN DUCK

(Histrionicus histrionicus)

MALE   FEMALE

COMMON NAME

Harlequin.

DESCRIPTION

Two forms of Harlequin occur in North America: the Eastern, *H. h. histrionicus*, and the Western, *H. h. pacificus*. The differences are insufficient to warrant separate treatment. The drake is a small, blue-backed bird with white spots or streaks on back, wings, sides of breast, neck, head and undertail coverts. The white markings are margined with black. Crown black with reddish streak on each side (*see sketch*). Sides of body and flanks, rich chestnut. The female is drab with whitish spots above, below and behind eye; whitish on upper breast. The bizarre, "stagy" appearance of the male accounts for its common name, "Harlequin" (buffoon), as well as its scientific name, *"Histrionicus"* (*histrio*, Latin: a stage player). The colors of the Eastern variety are stronger, the Western form being somewhat paler—more washed out.

Adult male in flight. Small size, swift flight, rapid wing beats and dark body, with reddish sides and curiously placed white spots and streaks, leave little room for confusion with any other species.

Adult male on water. Small size, "vivid white streaks on neck and breast, and chestnut flanks, conspicuous even in poor light," makes identification easy.

Adult female in flight. Small size, dark (drab) appearance, with whitish spots on head and whitish breast, *no white on wings*, will separate from much larger Surf Scoter.

Adult female on water. Small, buoyant, brownish duck with three white spots on head. Care is needed to separate it from the female Bufflehead, with one white spot, and the female Old Squaw, with whiter head and neck.

NORTHWARD MIGRATION

The Eastern Harlequin moves northward in small companies in February, March and April—according to latitude—from its wintering grounds along the Atlantic coast. These rarely extend farther south than Maine.

The Western Harlequin is much more abundant than the Eastern type. The wintering grounds reach from the Pribilofs and Aleutians to central California, and apparently much of the migration is from the coasts to nearby mountain streams along which it breeds. Brandt records northward migration taking place on May 20 in the Hooper Bay region of Alaska. The movement extends from February to May according to latitude.

COURTSHIP AND NESTING

Harlequins are spritely, playful and sociable birds—not noisy. The male, second in beauty only to the Wood Duck, is an ardent suitor. Courtship is accompanied by much head-bobbing and bowing by both sexes—a characteristic of sexually active ducks of all species. The drake throws the head back until the bill is pointing to the zenith and then jerks it forward with a cry, likened to the crowing of a rooster. At the same time the wings are partly expanded and drooped. Afterwards, the bird treads water and flaps its wings vigorously.

"They are sociable breeders, several pairs nesting together on rocky islands in the middle of rapidly flowing rivers." Nests are always close to water and are merely a depression in the ground scantily lined with grass, twigs and drab down from the female's breast. The nests may be sheltered under heather or scrub, in clefts in rocks or, occasionally, in the case of the Western subspecies, in holes in trees.

Five to eight—usually six or seven—creamy or light cinnamon-buff eggs are laid. They measure about 2.30 to 2.35 inches by 1.57 to 1.62 inches. Incubation period about 25 days.

FOOD

About 98 per cent animal matter, made up of crustaceans: 57; mollusks: 25; insects: 10; sea urchins: 2.5; and fishes: 2.5 per cent. The food habits render its flesh unpalatable and it is not hunted to any extent.

WEIGHTS

Griscom states the female is larger than the male, so it is doubtful whether the few records below are representative.

Male—*Average of 3:* 1 pound, 7 ounces. *Extremes:* 1 pound, 4 ounces to 1 pound, 9 ounces.

Female—*Average of 3:* 1 pound, 3½ ounces. *Extremes:* 1 pound, 1 ounce to 1 pound, 5 ounces.

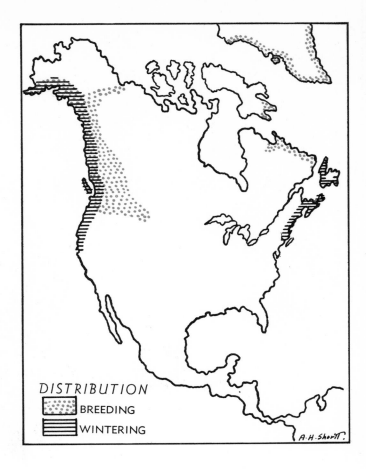

DISTRIBUTION
- [dotted] BREEDING
- [lined] WINTERING

A·H·Shortt.

DISTRIBUTION

Eastern Harlequin breeds in Iceland (resident), Greenland, southern Baffin Island, Labrador and Newfoundland. Casual in Europe and the British Isles. Winters on the Atlantic coast south to Maine—rarely to Long Island, New York.

Western Harlequin is found from Baikalia to Anadyr, Kamchatka, Kuriles, Sakhalin; also Pribilof and Aleutian Islands, and from Alaska south to the mountains of Montana, Wyoming, Colorado and central California. Winters mainly on the coast, and from the Pribilofs and Aleutians to central California; also on the Asiatic side from the Commander Islands to Japan.

REFERENCES

Brandt, Herbert, *Alaska Bird Trails*, 1943.
Forbush, Edward Howe, *Birds of Massachusetts and Other New England States* (Volume 1), 1925.
Kortright, Francis H., *The Ducks, Geese and Swans of North America*, 1942.
Witherby, Jourdain, Ticehurst and Tucker, *Handbook of British Birds* (Volume 3), 1943.
The A.O.U. Check-list of North American Birds (Fourth Edition), 1931.

Harlequin

MALLARD

(Anas platyrhynchos platyrhynchos)

MALE   FEMALE

COMMON NAMES

Greenhead, Wild Duck.

DESCRIPTION

A large, handsome, surface-feeding duck.

Adult male in flight. Large size; glossy, green head; chestnut breast; silvery-white belly; white wing linings; whitish edges to tail feathers; white bars fore and aft, of purplish-blue wing patch (speculum).

Adult male on water. Large size, glossy green head, yellow bill, white collar around neck (incomplete behind). Gray back with longitudinal dark bands; lighter gray sides; reddish orange legs, often visible in swimming.

Adult female in flight. Large, mottled-brown duck with white wing linings and whitish tail feathers; two white wing patch bars, as in male.

Adult female on water. Large, mottled-brown duck with orange bill and legs.

DISTRIBUTION

The whole of the Northern Hemisphere. Domesticated in many parts of the world, especially China, where it is an important source of meat, eggs and feathers.

In North America it breeds regularly from middle states north to Alaska and to the Arctic coast at the mouth of the Mackenzie River. More numerous west of the Mississippi and Hudson Bay.

Winters wherever open water occurs in the interior, sometimes even in Canada; on the Pacific coast from Bering Sea to Mexico; on the Atlantic coast, from the New England states to Mexico. Most abundant in the Mississippi Valley, Gulf coast and northern Mexico. Large numbers winter in Colorado, Utah, Illinois and other central states.

NORTHWARD MIGRATION

The hardy Mallard leads the van of migrating waterfowl, in late February and early March. First arrivals reach southern Alberta

49

about March 12; southern Saskatchewan, March 18 to 28; southern Manitoba, March 27 to 31. Peak migration: first ten days of April.

COURTSHIP AND NESTING

When they reach Canada, most Mallards are already paired. Courtship is a matter of much head-bobbing, sidling up to the female, breast displaying, and aerial flights, in which the male pursues the female, following her every turn and often touching wings. Several males may vie with each other in these pursuits, first one and then another seeking to take the lead and display his plumage to best advantage. A courting party crowds its members and the female so closely at times that their wings batter each other like a burst of machine gun fire. Finally, the female touches the male of her choice with her bill and the two fly off together. From then on they both join in ejecting intruders of the same species from the water area they pre-empt as their territory. Over this they will exercise sovereignty until incubation is well under way. Copulation takes place in the water.

Mallards are most versatile in choice of nesting locations—anywhere from the water's edge to two miles away. Sometimes Mallards take possession of old crow or hawk nests, up to fifty feet above ground. Nests usually are well concealed on the ground and constructed of surrounding vegetation, in a cavity made by the female, and are lined with down plucked by the female from her breast. This down appears to be developed especially for the purpose, as it is very loosely attached to the skin. When voluntarily leaving the nest, female covers the eggs with this warm blanket of down, which also serves to conceal them from predators, particularly the crow.

Clutch: Six to fifteen greenish-buff eggs, averaging 2.27 by 1.64 inches. Most frequent clutches: ten to twelve.

Incubation: 23 to 28 days, usually 24 days; by female only.

FOOD

Mostly vegetable matter: pondweeds, smartweeds, sedges, bulrush seeds, duck weeds, wild celery, wild rice, sagittaria, acorns; in fact, any good duck food available. On the plains, Mallards feed on the stubble fields of barley, wheat and corn. They take grasshoppers, mosquito larvae and other insects in substantial quantities.

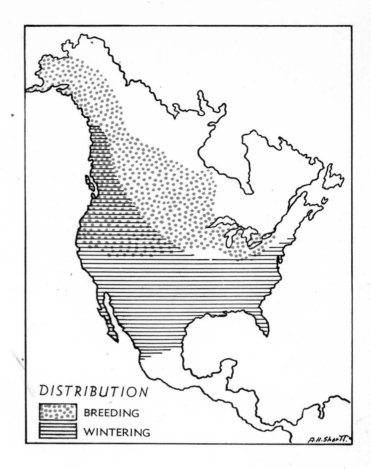

DISTRIBUTION

░░░ BREEDING

▤▤▤ WINTERING

WEIGHTS

Male—*Average of 1,577:* 2 pounds, 11 ounces. (Occasionally birds over 5 pounds are reported.)

Female—*Average of 1,177:* 2 pounds, 6 ounces.

SOUTHWARD MIGRATION

Fall migration is largely dependent on weather conditions. A limited movement south starts about the middle of September. A leisurely drift will continue until hard frosts close the sloughs, ponds and marshes. The Mallard is a hardy bird and he stays as long as food and water are available. Feeding extensively on waste grain on the stubble fields, Mallards show no inclination to leave until snow covers the ground. Mass migration from Canada takes place about November 5, when winter blasts from the north usually herald the final freeze-up.

Mallard

HOODED MERGANSER

(Lophodytes cucullatus)

MALE   FEMALE

COMMON NAMES

Sawbill, Fish Duck.

DESCRIPTION

The smallest of three mergansers found in North America. The striking black and white, fan-shaped crest distinguishes the male.

Adult male in flight. Small size, black and white markings on wings. The crest is depressed and shows as a white line sweeping back from the eye. The underparts are white. Flight, swift and quiet. The narrow bill gives the impression of a little black stick.

Adult male on water. Small size and conspicuous black-bordered white crest, which it is constantly fanning and depressing, should make identification easy. Two black stripes in front of wing, dividing the white of the breast, can readily be seen with a binocular.

Adult female in flight. Small size, brownish on back and chest. White on breast and belly; white speculum more reduced than in male.

Adult female on water. Small size; drab appearance; thin, buffy crest; pointed black bill and white speculum. Both sexes rise from the water with great speed.

DISTRIBUTION

A North American species. "Breeds locally in temperate North America from northern British Columbia, central Alberta, Manitoba, southern Ontario and New Brunswick to New York, central Pennsylvania, eastern South Carolina, central Florida, southern Tennessee, northern Arkansas, northern New Mexico, Oregon and Washington. Winters mainly in the southern states north to Massachusetts, Pennsylvania, Lake Michigan, Nebraska, Colorado, Utah, British Columbia and southeastern Alaska, and south to Cuba and central eastern Mexico. Accidental in Bermuda, Alaska, Wales and Ireland."

COURTSHIP AND NESTING

"In display, male's head (crest) is erected whole time. Main action is throwing of head far back and almost instantaneous return in a sweeping and graceful motion, note being delivered on forward movement while beak about vertical; on completion of movement bird propels itself suddenly forward for about fifteen feet." (W. H. Robb) F. Harper observed, in addition, the raising of the head several times in succession, with feathers on sides of head appearing puffed out, and dipping bill in water about three times, followed by rearing up on water, with or without wing flapping. Tail was kept slightly upturned and somewhat spread, and head was often turned repeatedly at right angles in approaching female.

"Nests in holes in trees growing in flooded areas adjoining great rivers, on shores of lakes and in swamps containing old and dead trees. The nest is usually inside a hollow tree or stump, or in a hole of any kind, sometimes open from above at any height; also exceptionally in hollow among roots of trees and in nesting boxes, or in a hollow fallen log. Little nesting material beyond down and feathers; occasionally a little moss and many chips of dead wood. The down is very delicate and soft, a very pale-gray—centers perhaps a little lighter."

Eggs—usually nine to twelve; very broad oval, almost spherical at times; pure white, smooth and very glossy, with extremely thick and hard shell. The eggs measure 2.11 by 1.77 inches.

FOOD

"Though this merganser does eat a certain amount of vegetable matter, its food comes mainly from the animal kingdom, and consists of small fishes, frogs, tadpoles, crayfish, beetles, caddis fly larvae and the like. It is an expert diver, is adept at chasing and catching small fish and obtains much of its food from the bottom of the fresh-water ponds and streams which it inhabits."

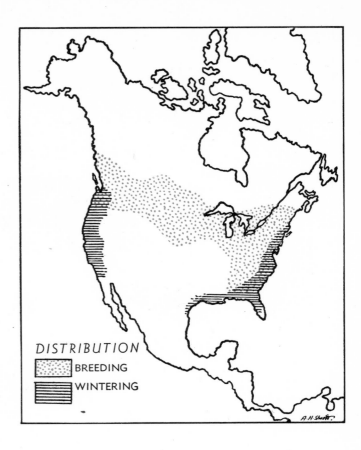

DISTRIBUTION
▫ BREEDING
▬ WINTERING

WEIGHTS

Male—*Average of 19:* 1 pound, 8 ounces. *Extremes:* 1 pound, 5 ounces to 1 pound, 15 ounces.

Female—*Average of 12:* 1 pound, 3½ ounces. *Extremes:* 1 pound to 1 pound, 7 ounces.

REFERENCES

Kortright, Francis H., *The Ducks, Geese and Swans of North America*, 1942.
Witherby, Jourdain, Ticehurst and Tucker, *Handbook of British Birds*, 1943.
The A.O.U. Check-list of North American Birds (Fourth Edition), 1931.

Hooded Merganser

OLD SQUAW

(Clangula hyemalis)

(ABOVE) MALE AND FEMALE IN WINTER.
(BELOW) MALE AND FEMALE IN SUMMER.

COMMON NAMES

Long-tailed Duck, Alewife (Scot.).

DESCRIPTION

A small, noisy, piebald diving duck with long central tail feathers (male). Female brown and white without long tail feathers.

Adult male in flight. Small size; rapid wing beats. Winter plumage is better known to sportsmen and bird students. The bird is mostly white with conspicuous black breast and wings. Central tail feathers greatly elongated. The summer (breeding) plumage is better known to Eskimos and far northern travelers. Head, neck, upper breast, wings and back are brownish-black. Whitish patch on side of head (variable in size), white lower breast and belly, long central tail feathers. Swift flight with much swerving and turning —more like shore birds than ducks—usually low over water in small, irregular formations. Have a habit of towering to great heights and then power diving with sizzling velocity—the wind screaming

through their wings. Usually plummet into the water with little finesse and a mighty splash. Sometimes, in a strong wind, they will head into the wind and glide in to alight in the normal manner of ducks. These latter remarks apply equally to the female.

Adult male on water. Small, neat black and white duck with small bill and very long central tail feathers. Full of life and chatter even on the most unpleasant winter days. Head, neck, upper back and most of body are white. Fore part of body is black. Ashy patch around eye, darker spot below and behind eye. Remarkable variety of call notes, gabblings and conversation. Some of the notes are quite musical. Bill is pinkish-orange, with black base and tip. Feet are bluish-gray with darker webs. In summer the head, neck, chest and back are brownish-black. An ashy-white face patch extends from the base of bill around the eye. Lower breast, sides, belly, flanks, under-tail coverts are white.

Adult female in flight. Brown-backed, *white-breasted*, black-winged, white-headed bird in winter plumage. In summer, the head and neck are variegated black and white. The neck and chest are darker, the sides whiter than in winter. In both plumages she lacks the long central tail feathers of the male.

Adult female on water. In winter, stocky, brown-backed, white-breasted and white-headed bird with small bill. In summer, head, neck and chest much darker. Whitish areas of head reduced to patch above and in front of eye and along sides of hinder part of neck.

COURTSHIP AND NESTING

The display may be seen before the birds leave for the north. Several males crowd around one female, bobbing the head and agitating the long tail feathers laterally as they are erected. Heads are thrown back and then snapped forward, at which time a call note is uttered. Males also sneak toward each other with outstretched necks and bills along the water, and there is much chasing.

On the breeding grounds the female is pursued by several males in wild courtship flights over the pond-studded tundra. She often plunges into the water, followed by the suitors, and swims beneath the surface for a considerable distance, reappearing in flight with the pack right behind. So on until she is exhausted, after which she rides quietly on a pond with the mate of her choice close by.

The nest is a cavity scratched out among grass, moss or gravel; lined with grasses and down; well concealed among the vegetation or sheltered by rocks. Six to eight eggs are the usual clutch, but up to eleven have been recorded. Clutches of greater number have been reported but are probably the product of more than one female. Eggs are smooth, grayish, buffy or greenish (olive). Incubation period about 24 days. Eggs measure 2.14 by 1.50 inches (average of fifty taken at Hooper Bay, Alaska, by Brandt).

FOOD

Dives for its food, often to considerable depth, remaining under water for half a minute or more. Almost 90 per cent is animal matter of which crustaceans, mollusks, insects and fishes are the items in order of importance. Grasses and pondweeds are the chief vegetable components. The flesh is tough and fishy and is not sought after.

WEIGHTS

Male—*Average of 21:* 1 pound, 13 ounces. *Extremes:* 1 pound, 9 ounces to 2 pounds, 5 ounces.

Female—*Average of 10:* 1 pound, 10 ounces. *Extremes:* 1 pound, 2 ounces to 1 pound, 12 ounces.

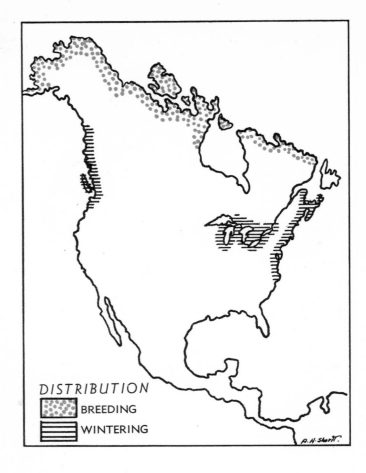

DISTRIBUTION
BREEDING
WINTERING

DISTRIBUTION

Circumpolar in the Northern Hemisphere. Breeds in Aleutian Islands, Alaska, the Arctic coasts and islands, the tundra, Greenland, Labrador, Iceland, Orkney and Shetland islands, Spitzbergen, northern Norway, Sweden, Finland and Russia; also the Arctic coasts and islands of Siberia. Winters in North America on both coasts and the Great Lakes; as far south as Washington state on the Pacific and North Carolina on the Atlantic. Winters also in Europe and Asia.

REFERENCES

Brandt, Herbert, *Alaska Bird Trails,* 1943.
Kortright, Francis H., *The Ducks, Geese and Swans of North America,* 1942.
Witherby, Jourdain, Ticehurst and Tucker, *Handbook of British Birds* (Volume 3), 1943.

Old Squaw

AMERICAN PINTAIL

(Anas acuta tzitzihoa)

FEMALE   MALE

COMMON NAMES

Sprig, Longneck.

DESCRIPTION

A handsome, streamlined, surface-feeding duck, second in numbers only to the Mallard. Continental population in 1945 estimated at about 20,000,000.

Adult male in flight. Large size; long, streamlined outline; brown head, white underparts and neck—white extends along sides of neck to head. Middle pair of tail feathers greatly elongated and pointed. Speculum (wing patch) shows a prominent white bar on the trailing edge.

Adult male on water. Large, slim, strikingly handsome bird with conspicuous white streak running up side of head. Cannot be mistaken for any other North American duck.

Adult female in flight. Large size, long neck, slim outline. Generally brownish with similar wing patch as male but colors much more subdued. Tail feathers buffy-white.

Adult female on water. Brownish bird, paler on sides of head; long, slim neck; gray bill and feet.

NORTHWARD MIGRATION

Pintails vie with Mallards to be first back on the Canadian breeding grounds. From the middle of March in southern Alberta to the last week of March in southern Saskatchewan and Manitoba, we look for the first Pintails, which are invariably paired birds. Migration is heavy and continuous throughout April, the later arrivals showing a preponderance of males. Large migrating flocks have been noted in Manitoba as late as May 10.

COURTSHIP AND NESTING

Males display on the water by throwing out their chests and curving their graceful necks until the bill rests on their white chests —much head-bobbing and gyrating to show off plumage.

Ecstatic pre-nuptial flights are indulged in by one, two or more males in pursuit of a female, who usually leads the party in wild, erratic courses. Hochbaum[1] describes how sometimes first one and then another male will fly ahead of the female and stall with the evident intent of showing his fine plumage to best advantage. Occasionally a male will grasp the belly feathers of the female in mid-air and hang·on until they are in danger of crashing.

Nests invariably are on dry ground anywhere from the water's edge to a mile or more away. Concealment is a matter of indifference —some nests are well concealed among vegetation, others are wide open to the sky on stubble or even bare plowing. Egg clutch varies from five to eleven—average seven. Eggs average 2.16 by 1.50 inches and are pale olive-green when freshly laid. Average brood: six. Seven years of brood counts by Ducks Unlimited's keemen recorded 60,700 females with 365,385 young, an average so close to six that the difference is negligible.

Incubation period: 22–23 days; by females only.

FOOD

Vegetable matter forms 90 per cent of the adult Pintail's food. Pondweeds, sedges and grasses are most favored, but in recent years this species has joined the Mallards in feeding extensively on waste grain on the farm fields. During the first two or three weeks of their lives, young Pintails feed almost exclusively on aquatic and upland insect life. On the land they catch insects with remarkable dexterity.

WEIGHTS

Male—*Average of 234 adults:* 2.27 pounds. *Average of 390 juveniles:* 2.04 pounds.

Female—*Average of 63 adults:* 1.95 pounds. *Average of 218 juveniles:* 1.82 pounds.

SOUTHWARD MIGRATION

There is an important migration of Pintails from northern Canada, and from the prairies, to the Pacific coast. An early movement takes place in late July from the central plains. A majority of the birds migrate in October, but considerable numbers linger in Canada until frost closes the ponds and marshes in late October or early November. A relatively small number migrate to the Hawaiian islands, a journey which involves an ocean flight of 2,000 miles.

---

[1] Hochbaum, H. Albert, *The Canvasback on a Prairie Marsh*, 1944.

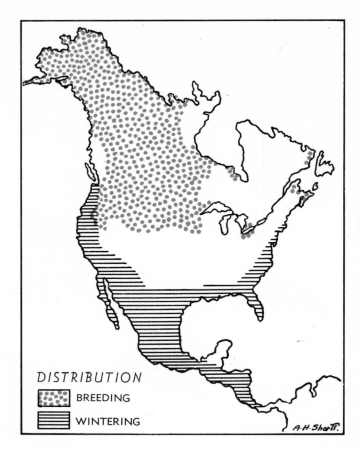

DISTRIBUTION

▒ BREEDING

≡ WINTERING

A.H.Shortt.

Some reach Palmyra island, south and west of Hawaii, 3,000 miles from the American mainland. The southern migration is drawn out and widespread across the continent, chiefly along the Mississippi, central and Pacific flyways.

DISTRIBUTION

Most wide-ranging of all North American ducks. Pintails are circumpolar in distribution, the American form having sub-specific status. They breed chiefly west of the Mississippi from the midwestern states to the Rockies and mountain valleys, north to the Arctic coast at Queen Maud Gulf, Mackenzie River delta, Alaska and islands of the Bearing Sea. Recently established (or re-established) as breeders in Nova Scotia, New Brunswick and Labrador. They winter on the Pacific slope from southern British Columbia south to Central America and from Delaware to Florida. The wintering range is practically continuous throughout the southern states, Mexico (excepting Yucatan peninsula) and the Central American republics to Panama.

A.H. Shortt. 1946

American Pintail

REDHEAD

(Aythya americana)

MALE   FEMALE

DESCRIPTION

A large, red-headed, black-chested, gray-backed diving duck with bluish-gray bill and feet. Females generally brownish above, with pale brown head and neck which fades as season advances.

Adult male in flight. Large, puffy-headed duck with heavy-looking body, showing black chest in sharp contrast with white breast. The head and neck appear short compared with the Canvasback—the only species with which it is likely to be confused.

Adult male on water. Appears as large as Mallard or Canvasback. Reddish-chestnut head with high brow contour separates it readily from the similarly (less intensely) colored low-brow-contoured (wedge-shaped) head of the Canvasback. Dark gray back and sides.

Adult female in flight. Large size, head shape and general brownish appearance of head, back and wings with dull-grayish wing patches and white breast, will separate it from the similarly colored females of the Canvasback and Lesser Scaup.

Adult female on water. Large size with high brow contour and puffy head. Pale brown color of head serves to distinguish her from female Scaup or Ring-necked Ducks.

DISTRIBUTION

Breeds discontinuously from southern British Columbia, northern Alberta (Athabasca delta), central Saskatchewan (Cumberland House district), central Manitoba (the Pas marshes), south and east to western Pennsylvania (Pymatuning), southeastern Michigan, southern Wisconsin, northern Iowa, southern Minnesota, central Nevada, and southern California. Winters from southern British Columbia south on the Pacific slope to southern California and the southern tier of states to the Gulf coast of Texas south through Mexico; and on the Atlantic coast from Delaware to North Carolina.

NORTHWARD MIGRATION

Arrives in southern Canada about April 10 to 15. Northward movement is well behind the retreating snowline.

COURTSHIP AND NESTING

The first Redheads to arrive in Canada in mid-April are mated birds, but there is a preponderance of males in the later arrivals. Hochbaum found the sex ratio to be 56 males to 44 females in four years' observations on the Delta Marshes in Manitoba.

The courtship flights are similar to those of the Canvasback, the female leading a wild chase over the marsh with the male following her every dip, zoom and turn with reckless speed. The male frequently seizes the tail feathers of the female in his bill and, as Hochbaum expresses it, literally "cracks the whip" as she swerves to dislodge her suitor. On the water, the usual "head throws, neck stretches, sneaks and mild combats between rival males take place."

The nesting of the Redhead is a curious and complicated business. In Manitoba they nest over water in bulrush, cattail or other emergent or semi-aquatic vegetation. A dry-land nest is a rarity, but in southern Alberta (Brooks district) fully 50 per cent of Redhead nests are on dry land—close to water. There is little effort at concealment. Their nests over water are soundly constructed from the material in which they are situated, but their dry-land nests are of weed stems and debris with copious whitish down from the female's breast.

The eggs, usually ten to fifteen, are olive-buff and measure 2.64 by 1.79 inches. Incubation period 22 to 24 days. Surplus eggs are deposited in other nests of their own or other species. In the Brooks district of Alberta, Randall found Redhead eggs in the nests of Mallard, Pintail, Blue-winged Teal, Gadwall, Lesser Scaup, White-winged Scoter, Ruddy Duck and even Canada Goose. Sometimes several Redhead females will deposit surplus eggs in one nest, either of their own or other species, so that the original owner is forced to abandon the nest. These so-called "dump nests" may contain anywhere from 18 to 32 eggs which, although fertile, never hatch. A few (rarely) which have been deposited in the nests of other species hatch, which accounts for the occasional observation of one or two Redhead young in broods of other species.

FOOD

The Redhead is a diving duck and procures most of its food in that manner. Ninety per cent of its food is aquatic plants, leaves, seeds, roots, and the balance mollusks and insects. Baldpates, Coots and Gadwall often attend the diving Redhead to partake of the fruits of its industry and repay by warning the Redhead of danger.

WEIGHTS

Male—*Average of 70:* 2 pounds, 8 ounces. *Extremes:* 1 pound, 14 ounces to 3 pounds.

Female—*Average of 26:* 2 pounds, 4 ounces. *Extremes:* 1 pound, 6 ounces to 2 pounds, 11 ounces.

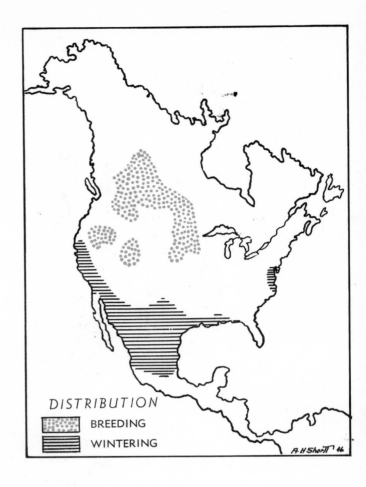

DISTRIBUTION

[ ] BREEDING

[ ] WINTERING

SOUTHWARD MIGRATION

Redheads depart from Canada about mid-October with little regard for weather conditions. There is a migration route through Eastern Canada to the Atlantic coast and another one from the western prairies to British Columbia and the Pacific coast. A regular route is down the Mississippi flyway to the southern states and Mexico. Banding returns of Ducks Unlimited show the species to be under the heaviest shooting pressure (14 per cent) of any species—a figure which confirms the banding results from the Bear River marshes, Utah, of 13.3 per cent.

The vulnerable nesting habits, discontinuous breeding and migratory habits, and apparent susceptibility to gunning is such that special concern is felt for the Redhead. It has shown less resilience to adverse conditions than any other species, with the possible exception of the Ruddy Duck.

REFERENCES

Hochbaum, H. Albert, *The Canvasback on a Prairie Marsh*, 1944.

Kortright, Francis H., *The Ducks, Geese and Swans of North America*, 1942.

Todd, W. E. Clyde, *Birds of Western Pennsylvania*, 1940.

Williams, Cecil S., "Migration of the Redhead from the Utah Breeding Grounds," *The Auk*, Volume 61, Number 2 (April, 1944), pages 251-9.

"The A.O.U. Check-list of North American Birds" (20th Supplement), *The Auk*, Volume 62, Number 3 (July, 1945), page 438.

A.H. Shortt, 1946.

Redhead

RING-NECKED DUCK

(Aythya collaris)

MALE   FEMALE

COMMON NAMES

Blackhead, Blackjack, Ringbill, Raft Duck.

DESCRIPTION

A medium-sized diving duck with tufty black head and back, easily confused with the Lesser Scaup (Bluebill).

Adult male in flight. Black head and chest with white underparts are similar to the markings of the Scaups and Redhead, but the lack of broad white wing patches, as in the Scaups, and the black head will separate it from those species. Under favorable light conditions a narrow white margin on the trailing edge of the wing, and the black head and back, are the best field marks.

Adult male on water. Black head and back, grayish-white sides with prominent white crescent between sides and black chest, white ring around bill near tip, are distinguishing field marks. The ring around the bill is visible for surprisingly long distances with good

binoculars. The chestnut collar around the neck is not visible in the field.

Adult female in flight. Difficult to tell from female Scaups or Redhead. Most reliable clue is to see her with her male.

Adult female on water. White ring around bill is easily seen with aid of binoculars. Whitish face patches are also visible in good light. Both are good field marks.

NORTHWARD MIGRATION

Arrives in southern Canada about mid-April with Lesser Scaups, Redheads and Canvasbacks. Rarely seen in large flocks—usually mated pairs or small parties of half a dozen or so pairs.

COURTSHIP AND NESTING

Roberts states, "When settled on the water the dark females and lighter males keep close together in pairs, and there is much agitation and grotesque display as the courtship progresses. The males dash about in short spurts, splashing the water behind them, or swim rapidly around with the neck extended and arched and the feathers of the crown erected, forming a noticeable, bushy, occipital crest."

Contrary to reiterated statements in current bird books, the Ring-necked Duck is not a common breeder on the prairies; in fact, it is rarely encountered. The breeding range lies largely north of the agricultural belt in the parklands along the edge of the Pre-Cambrian shield. The nest is a fairly bulky structure made of the materials in which it is located in marsh or muskeg, lined with finer grasses and well concealed in slough grasses, rushes or cattails. Invariably surrounded by or over water—so far as the writer knows. Six to twelve eggs of greenish-white or greenish-buff color are laid. They measure 2.26 by 1.57 inches. Incubation period is unknown but probably 22 to 24 days. The eggs are protected by dark gray down from the female's breast.

FOOD

Vegetable matter forms 80 per cent of the Ring-neck's food. The principal items are water lilies, pondweeds, sedges, grasses, smartweeds, muskgrass and other common aquatics. Insects, mollusks and tadpoles make up the bulk of its animal diet. Although smaller, it is considered by wild game epicures to be equal in flavor to the famed Canvasback and superior to the Bluebill. It prefers the freshwater ponds rather than the coastal marshes.

SOUTHWARD MIGRATION

Leaves Canada in October with the Redheads and Canvasbacks —usually ahead of the Bluebills (Lesser Scaups), although heavy migrations are seen some years in the first few days of November, particularly through the evergreen regions of eastern Manitoba. The direction of the flight is southeast. There is no great migration of this species through the prairies. They seem to follow along the southern edge of the coniferous forests in both their southern and northern movements.

DISTRIBUTION

Breeds from northwestern Pennsylvania (Pymatuning), Maine, Prince Edward Island, southern New Brunswick, western Nova

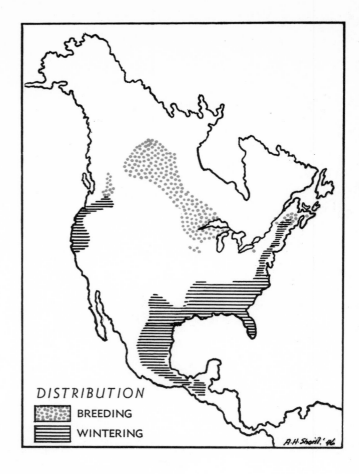

DISTRIBUTION

▒ BREEDING

≡ WINTERING

Scotia, Quebec, southwestern Ontario, northern Michigan, Wisconsin, Minnesota, central Manitoba, northern Saskatchewan, northern Alberta, central Mackenzie valley and south-central British Columbia; south (rarely or formerly) to south-central Oregon, northern Utah, northern Nebraska, northern Iowa and northern Illinois. Winters from southern British Columbia to New Mexico, Arkansas and Texas, and from Massachusetts south in interior freshwater ponds and reservoirs to West Virginia, Florida and the Bahamas; through Mexico to Guatemala.

REFERENCES

Forbush, Edward Howe, *Birds of Massachusetts and Other New England States*, 1925.
Hochbaum, H. Albert, *The Canvasback on a Prairie Marsh*, 1944.
Kortright, Francis H., *The Ducks, Geese and Swans of North America*, 1942.
Mendall, Howard L., "Ring-neck Duck Breeding in Eastern North America," *The Auk*, Volume 55 (July, 1938), pages 401-4.
Roberts, Thomas S., *Birds of Minnesota*, 1932.
Todd, W. E. Clyde, *Birds of Western Pennsylvania*, 1940.
"The A.O.U. Check-list of North American Birds" (20th Supplement), *The Auk*, Volume 62, Number 3 (July, 1945), page 438.

Ring=necked Duck

RUDDY DUCK

(Oxyura jamaicensis rubida)

MALE   FEMALE

COMMON NAMES

Spiketail, Ruddy.

DESCRIPTION

A small, thick-necked diving duck. Male in summer reddish-chestnut on back; black crown; white cheek patches and bright blue bill. White underneath. Female is dark brown on back and darker on crown, with mottled white cheek patches. Bill, dusky. Whitish underparts.

Adult male in flight. Summer plumage: a small reddish-chestnut duck with short, thick neck; black crown; white cheek patches and bright blue bill. White underparts. Readily identified at long distances. Winter plumage: crown, nape and back dark brown—darker on head. Cheeks and chin, white; underparts white—more or less barred with chestnut or rusty stains. Bill, blue but less brilliant.

Adult male on water. Summer plumage: a perky reddish-chestnut duck with black crown, conspicuous white cheek patches

and bright blue bill. Rides buoyantly in proud, cocky manner with tail often tilted up over the back. Winter plumage: dark brown crown and back, with white cheeks and blue bill—as in summer, though less bright.

Adult female in flight. Chunky, short-necked brownish duck with white underparts, white cheeks divided by a dark stripe and dusky bluish bill. Same in summer and winter.

Adult female on water. Small, dark brown duck with stiff, longish tail often uptilted. Whitish cheeks appear mottled. Bill, dusky, looks large in proportion to other features. This latter applies to both male and female.

DISTRIBUTION

Confined to North America. "Breeds from central British Columbia, Alberta, and northern Manitoba to western Minnesota, southeastern Wisconsin, southeastern Michigan, northern Illinois, northern Iowa, central Texas, northern New Mexico, central Arizona and northern Lower California; reported to have bred sporadically in Ungava, Maine, Massachusetts (Cape Cod), Rhode Island and central New York; and breeding colonies have been found in southern Lower California, the Valley of Mexico and Guatemala. Winters on the Atlantic coast from Chesapeake Bay (more rarely from Massachusetts) to Florida, the Bahamas and West Indies; on the Pacific coast from southern British Columbia to Lower California, Guatemala and Costa Rica; and in the interior from central Arizona, southern Illinois and western Pennsylvania southward. Casual or accidental in Bermuda, Nova Scotia, New Brunswick and Alaska. (A closely allied race occurs in Puerto Rico, Haiti and Jamaica.)"

COURTSHIP AND NESTING

The Ruddy Duck is peculiar in many respects. It does not undergo an eclipse plumage after breeding, but the male has a distinct summer and winter plumage. He stays with the female (who alone incubates the eggs) and assists in the care of the young. It is said to raise two broods in the southern parts of its breeding range, but I have never seen conclusive evidence of this. Although small, it lays the largest egg of all the diving ducks, exclusive of the eiders and scoters. Its courtship display is one of the most elaborate of all. The male—often several together—swims proudly around a female, with chest puffed out and head thrown back until it almost touches his uptilted tail. From time to time he beats his bright blue bill on his chest, hitting the water at the same time in a rapid tattoo. Lowering his tail to act as an aquaplane, he rushes through the water, beating forward with his feet for a short distance. An encounter with a rival results in a spirited rough-and-tumble, until one or the other is driven away. The sound made by these water splurges is so characteristic that the cause can be correctly identified without seeing the birds at all. When alarmed, the Ruddy has the grebelike ability to submerge slowly. Its favorite nesting place is in the deeper prairie sloughs or secluded marshes, where open water and dense growths of cattail and bulrush are found. The nest is constructed above water, often domed over, and is a neatly woven, basketlike structure. The remarkably large eggs—average 2.45 by 1.79 inches—are pure white or creamy, thick-shelled, rough and granular, sometimes misshapen but generally ovate. Clutches vary from three to fourteen or more, but six to eight are more common in Canada. Hochbaum states, "Many fresh Ruddy eggs collected from incomplete clutches show an incubation period of 21 to 22 days in the incubator." The Ruddy sometimes constructs more than one nest and uses one in which to deposit surplus eggs, but rarely drops eggs into other ducks' nests.

FOOD

About 75 per cent is vegetable matter—pondweeds and bulrush predominating. The balance is insects and other aquatic animal life.

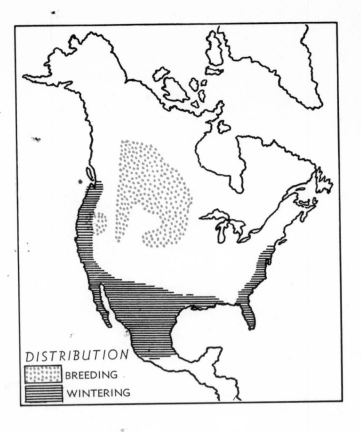

DISTRIBUTION

▦ BREEDING
▤ WINTERING

WEIGHTS

Male—*Average of 8:* 1 pound, 5½ ounces. *Extremes:* 1 pound, 3 ounces to 1 pound, 12 ounces.

Female—*Average of 8:* 1 pound, 2 ounces. *Extremes:* 11 ounces to 1 pound, 7 ounces.

MIGRATIONS

The Ruddy is one of the last to arrive on its breeding grounds in Canada and one of the last to start nesting. The last week in April sees the first arrivals. The main fall migration takes place about the middle of September, although a few remain until freeze-up.

REFERENCES

Hochbaum, H. Albert, *The Canvasback on a Prairie Marsh*, 1944.
Kortright, Francis H., *The Ducks, Geese and Swans of North America*, 1942.
The A.O.U. Check-list of North American Birds (Fourth Edition), 1931.

Ruddy Duck

GREATER SCAUP

(Aythya marila)

MALE   FEMALE

COMMON NAMES

Big Bluebill, Bay Broadbill, Bay Blackhead.

DESCRIPTION

A medium-sized diving duck with black head, neck and chest; white breast; sooty brown belly. General effect similar to Lesser Scaup (little Bluebill), except head and neck glossed with greenish instead of purplish.

Adult male in flight. A medium-sized black and white duck with a *broad white wing patch* on the trailing edge of wing. This patch is about twice as long as that of the otherwise similarly patterned Lesser Scaup and may be clearly seen when the bird is "going away" as it takes off from the water.

Adult male on water. Indistinguishable from the Lesser Scaup. Black head, neck and chest; bright blue bill; white sides and whitish back; dark rear end—describes both species. Under exceptionally favorable light conditions the greenish gloss on the head may be seen. The gloss on the Lesser Scaup is purplish. Since these are lustrous metallic colors, they vary with the angle of incidence.

Adult female in flight. Medium size; generally brownish appearance with white breast and belly shading to brown towards tail. White face patch around base of bill. White wing patch as in male but not quite so long. Otherwise indistinguishable from Lesser Scaup.

Adult female on water. Cannot be told apart from Lesser Scaup. The habit of Greater Scaups on migration and on the wintering grounds of rafting in huge flocks in the larger freshwater lakes and saltwater bays, well offshore in the daytime, is a good clue to their identity.

NORTHWARD MIGRATION

Starts to move northward along the coasts in February and March. Leaves the wintering grounds early in April. Arrives in force on its Alaskan breeding grounds about May 24. Its passage through

Canada is not well known but evidently follows routes north of the prairies.

COURTSHIP AND NESTING

"The male Scaup anxious to pair approaches the female with head and neck held up to their fullest extent, the bill being raised in the air to an angle of 50 or 60 degrees. If the female responds to this, she also lifts the neck stiffly, at the same time uttering a crooning note. If alarmed, or pretending to be so, she swims away quickly with powerful strokes, uttering her quacking cry. When paired, the female often comes up to the male and bows her head gently several times. The actual show of the male is a quick throw up of the head and neck, which is greatly swollen with air as it extends. At the summit of extension, the bird utters a gentle cry, like the words *pawhoo*, only uttered once. As he makes this show, the female sometimes swims around him, lowering the head and dipping the bill in the surface of the water and making a gentle call. . . . The male also utters a very low whistle. Except the harsh, loud cry of the female, all these calls of pairing Scaup are very low in tone, and the spectator must be within a few yards of the birds to hear them.

"The nest is usually placed not far from water and consists of a depression in the ground, lined with grasses and down. From five to twenty-two eggs have been found in the nests, but the larger number were probably the product of more than one female, since the usual number seems to be seven to ten. Color olive buff; size 2.46 by 1.72 inches."

FOOD

Diet averages fifty-fifty animal and vegetable matter. Mollusks (including oysters), insects, crustaceans and small fish make up the animal food. Pondweeds, muskgrass, water milfoils, sedges, grasses (including wild rice) and wild celery are the important vegetable foods.

WEIGHTS

Male—*Average of 24:* 2 pounds, 1 ounce. *Extremes:* 1 pound, 5 ounces to 2 pounds, 10 ounces.

Female—*Average of 18:* 2 pounds. *Extremes:* 1 pound, 5 ounces to 2 pounds, 15 ounces.

The weights of small Greater Scaup overlap with those of large Lesser Scaup, so cannot be used as a reliable guide for identification.

SOUTHWARD MIGRATION

One of the last of the migrants to come out of the north. They raft in thousands on Lake Winnipeg several miles offshore in late October, where they are taken frequently in fishermen's nets. They

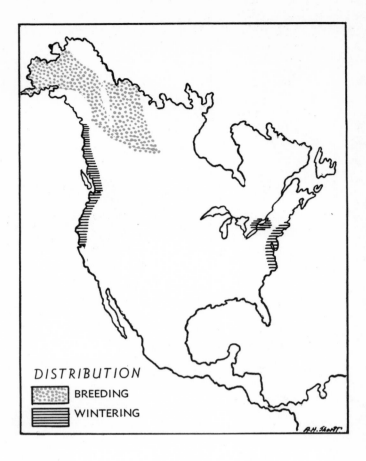

DISTRIBUTION
BREEDING
WINTERING

do not come into the marshes to feed and rarely appear in hunters' bags. They leave Manitoba in November, when freeze-up of the big waters is imminent, and head southeast towards the Great Lakes and Atlantic coast.

DISTRIBUTION

Breeds in Arctic Europe (also northern Scotland, the Outer Hebrides and Iceland), Arctic Asia and from the Aleutian islands, Alaska and northwestern Canada to the west coast of Hudson Bay —more common in the west. Winters south to the Mediterranean, Black and Caspian Seas and India (rarely). In America, from the Aleutian Islands south to northern Lower California and (occasionally) Colorado, Nevada, New Mexico and Arizona; also from the Great Lakes and Maine south on the Atlantic coast to North Carolina and on the Gulf coasts of Florida, Louisiana and Texas.

REFERENCES

Brandt, Herbert, *Alaska Bird Trails,* 1943.
Coward, T. A., *Birds of Wayside and Woodland,* 1936.
Kortright, Francis H., *The Ducks, Geese and Swans of North America,* 1942.
Smythies, R. W., *Birds of Burma,* 1940.
Todd, W. E. Clyde, *Birds of Western Pennsylvania,* 1940.
The A.O.U. Check-list of North American Birds (Fourth Edition), 1931.
——— (20th Supplement), *The Auk,* Volume 62, Number 3 (July, 1945), page 438.

Greater Scaup

LESSER SCAUP

(Aythya affinis)

MALE   FEMALE

COMMON NAMES

Bluebill, Broadbill, Fall Duck, Raft Duck, Blackhead.

DESCRIPTION

A medium-sized black and white duck with bright blue bill. Found only in North America.

Adult male in flight. Medium size, short neck, tufty head. Black head, neck and chest; white underbody. Dark wings with broad white wing patch on the secondaries. The Greater Scaup's wing patch extends into the adjoining five or six primaries (*see sketch*).

WING OF GREATER SCAUP   WING OF LESSER SCAUP
COMPARISON OF THE EXTENT OF WHITE ON THE FLIGHT FEATHERS
OF THE WINGS

Adult male on water. Medium size, tufty black head, bright blue bill. Shows large amount of white on sides and back—not apparent. in flight. Purplish luster on head. Indistinguishable from Greater Scaup.

Adult female in flight. Medium size, general brownish color, blue bill with white patch on face at base of bill. Whitish underbody and white wing patch. Smaller size of white wing patch is only reliable distinguishing feature compared with Greater Scaup.

Adult female on water. Medium size, brownish head, neck and back. Blue bill with conspicuous white patch around base of bill —a feature also carried by juveniles of both sexes.

NORTHWARD MIGRATION

Arrives in southern prairie provinces of Canada in mid-April and spreads northward as rapidly as waters open up. Principal nesting areas are in parklands between agricultural belt and Pre-Cambrian shield. Arrives in waves, and first arrivals are paired birds. Sex ratio—67 males to 33 females (average of four years of records by Hochbaum at Delta Waterfowl Research Station, Delta, Manitoba).

COURTSHIP AND NESTING

Spectacular courting flights, with several males in pursuit of a female, are carried out with dizzy speed and dazzling changes in height and direction. On the water the usual head-bobbing, neck-stretching and love notes are given by rival males and responded to, on occasion, by the female. The male, after pairing has taken place and territory chosen, is very aggressive in chasing away intruding males; but, curiously, mated pairs often tolerate a sexually nonactive male, which consorts with the pair on amicable terms.

The Lesser Scaup is a late nester, rarely starting before May 20. Nests with fresh eggs are frequently found in early August—probably second attempts. The nests are well-concealed cavities near marshes, sloughs and ponds—often in wet places but more often on dry land near water. They are lined with fine grasses and well supplied with down from the female's breast. The clutch of eggs is usually ten or twelve, but varies from six to fifteen. Eggs measure 2.25 by 1.56 inches (average) and are dark olive-buff in color. Incubation period: 22–23 days.

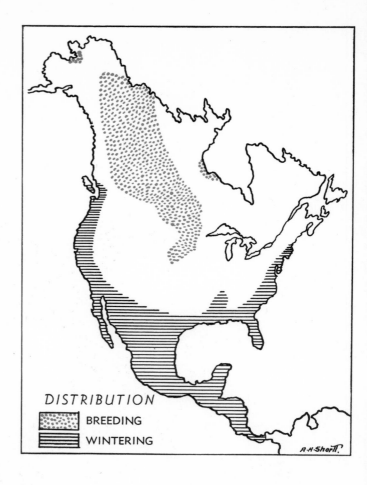

DISTRIBUTION

▒ BREEDING

≡ WINTERING

R-H-Shortt.

FOOD

Stomach analysis of 1,051 specimens taken in all months of the year revealed that 59.55 per cent of the food was vegetable matter. Pondweeds, grasses (including wild rice), sedges, wild celery, musk grass, coontail and smartweeds were preferred foods. The balance of animal matter was made up of mollusks: 25 per cent; insects: 12 per cent; crustaceans: 1.34 per cent and miscellaneous: 2.13 per cent.

WEIGHTS

Male—*Average of 112:* 1 pound, 14 ounces. *Extremes:* 1 pound, 6 ounces to 2 pounds, 5 ounces.

Female—*Average of 118:* 1 pound, 12 ounces. *Extremes:* 1 pound, 3 ounces to 2 pounds, 2 ounces.

SOUTHWARD MIGRATION

This late-maturing species gathers in large numbers in the park-land lakes north of the agricultural belt, where the birds find an abundance of food. In August great concentrations can be seen from the air in favored locations. They are made up largely of flightless (molting) adults and maturing juveniles. The southward migration starts early in October, but mass exodus does not take place until freeze-up, usually about the first week in November.

DISTRIBUTION

Breeds from the north-central states and southeastern Ontario, north through the prairie provinces of Canada and southern British Columbia, to the west coast of Hudson Bay across to eastern Alaska and the Mackenzie Delta.

REFERENCES

Cottam, Clarence, "Food Habits of North American Diving Ducks," *U.S. Department of Agriculture Technical Bulletin 643*, 1939.
Hochbaum, H. Albert, *The Canvasback on a Prairie Marsh*, 1944.
Kortright, Francis H., *The Ducks, Geese and Swans of North America*, 1942.
The A.O.U. Check-list of North American Birds (Fourth Edition), 1931.
——— (20th Supplement), *The Auk*, Volume 62, Number 3 (July, 1945), page 438.

Lesser Scaup

AMERICAN SCOTER

(Oidemia nigra americana)

MALE   FEMALE

COMMON NAMES

Sea or Bay Coot, Black Duck.

DESCRIPTION

More ducklike than other scoters. The male is all black except for orange-yellow protuberance at base of bill. The female is all brown except for darker crown and whitish cheeks, throat and chin.

Adult male in flight. All-black, medium-sized duck with silvery sheen to flight feathers. Neater outline (not so heavy-bodied as the other scoters). The only completely black native duck.

Adult male on water. Medium-sized, glossy-black body unrelieved by any color other than the orange-yellow protuberance at base of bill. Rides buoyantly and carries bill either horizontal or tilted up. Groups of males, when approached by boat, crowd closely together and move this way and that as one bird with their bills pointing upwards—a characteristic of the species.

Adult female in flight. Medium-sized, all-brown body with silvery sheen to flight feathers. White cheeks and throat may be seen at close range but may be confused with female Surf Scoter. Outline more ducklike.

Adult female on water. Rides buoyantly and has the same habit of holding the bill straight out or tilted up. All brown, darker on crown and with whitish cheeks, throat and chin. Neater, more ducklike outline than other scoters.

DISTRIBUTION

Breeds from northeastern Siberia and Mackenzie Bay to the Bering Sea coast of Alaska, the Aleutian and Kuril Islands, James Bay and Newfoundland. Winters on the Atlantic coast from Maine and more rarely Newfoundland to New Jersey, and irregularly to South Carolina and Florida; and on the Pacific from the Pribilof and Aleutian Islands to southern California, and from the Commander Islands to Japan and China; south in the interior to the Great Lakes and irregularly to Wyoming, Colorado and Louisiana.

COURTSHIP AND NESTING

Little information is available on the courtship habits of the American Scoter; but they probably are similar to those of the type species, the Common Scoter (*O. n. nigra*), on which A. Brooks remarks, "In display, male scuttles along surface for a few yards, head almost under water, making the rattling note, or raises forepart of body out of water with head carried high, tail cocked up and bill open, uttering the whistling note. . . . Chasing between both sexes also occurs and W. Brewster also notes a sort of revolving dance, all members of a flock following one another closely as they swim around and around in great circle, each bird using feet so energetically as to keep most of its body above surface."

Brandt records that in the Hooper Bay district of Alaska the American Scoter is one of the last migrants to arrive and nest. The first nest found was June 23, and the height of season for fresh clutches was between this date and July 1. Nests were found in clumps of dried grasses of the previous year along dune ridges and embankments bordering estuaries, although the birds were also present on the rolling tundra. The nest is skillfully hidden in the largest available grass clump. An excavation is made and lined with grasses and smoky-gray down. Five to eight eggs are laid, and they measure 2.65 by 1.82 inches (Brandt: average of 35). The color shows considerable variation between sets. The shells are translucent; and, in freshly laid eggs, the golden yolk lends a pinkish tint to yellow-white, cinnamon-pink, or semi-ivory colors.

MIGRATIONS

Least abundant of the three scoters. The height of the spring migration along the Atlantic coast is in April and early May. The fall migration extends from the beginning of September, when the first arrivals are all males, and reaches its height in October, when the birds of the year come down. The pattern along the Pacific coast is similar. Arrival on the breeding grounds starts about the middle of May and becomes general the first week of June.

FOOD

Ninety per cent of the food is animal matter, of which mollusks —mussels, clams, oysters, scallops—form the bulk. Pondweeds and musk grass are favored items in the 10 per cent vegetable diet.

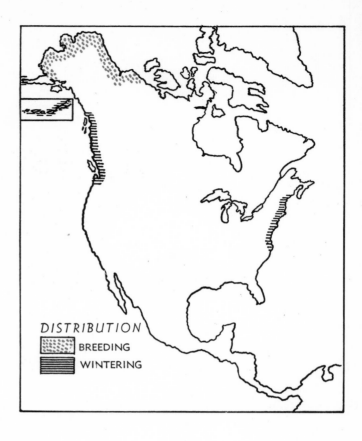

DISTRIBUTION
▓ BREEDING
☰ WINTERING

WEIGHTS

Male—*Average of 7: 2 pounds, 8 ounces. Extremes: 2 pounds, 3 ounces to 2 pounds, 13 ounces.*

Female—*Average of 2: 2 pounds, 3 ounces. Extremes: 1 pound, 15 ounces to 2 pounds, 7 ounces.*

REFERENCES

Brandt, Herbert, *Alaska Bird Trails*, 1943.
Kortright, Francis H., *The Ducks, Geese and Swans of North America*, 1942.
Witherby, Jourdain, Ticehurst and Tucker, *Handbook of British Birds* (Volume 3), 1943.
The A.O.U. Check-list of North American Birds (Fourth Edition), 1931.

American Scoter

SURF SCOTER

(Melanitta perspicillata)

MALE   FEMALE

COMMON NAMES

Sea or Bay Coot, Scooter.

DESCRIPTION

Large, all-black sea duck with *conspicuous white patches on forehead, hindhead and nape.* Female brownish above, lighter below. Head with black crown and whitish patches below eye, around ear and hindhead.

Adult male in flight. Medium-sized, heavy-bodied, all-black duck with long head, on the forehead and nape of which there are conspicuous white patches. Wing linings are black. Flies in flocks of twenty to forty without regular formation, or in very large flocks on migration. A loud humming of the wings can be heard at surprising distances.

Adult male on water. Medium-sized, all-black duck with conspicuous white patches on forehead and nape. The nape patch tapers off to a point at base. The varicolored bill—different in shape from other scoters—forms a straight line with head as in Canvasback, giving the head an elongated appearance. A black spot on side of bill, bordered behind with red and in front with white and orange, makes a striking field mark at close range. Yearling males resemble the females and lack the white head patches.

Adult female in flight. Medium-sized, all-black (brownish) appearance without silvery sheen on underwings. Two whitish patches on head help to identify. Immatures of both sexes are paler below—almost white on the belly.

Adult female on water. Medium-sized, thickset body, with two whitish patches on side of head fore and aft of the eye, and whitish patch (inconstant) on nape serve to distinguish.

DISTRIBUTION

Breeds from northwestern Alaska and casually Greenland, south to the Gulf of St. Lawrence, James Bay, Mackenzie and the interior of the Ungava peninsula; probably also in northern Manitoba,

89

northern Saskatchewan and Alberta. Winters on the Atlantic coast from the Bay of Fundy to Florida and on the Pacific from the Aleutian Islands to Lower California; also on the Great Lakes and sparingly in the interior of southern British Columbia and in Louisiana. Casual in Bermuda, Great Britain, France, Finland, Scandinavia, Belgium, Holland, and on Bering Island.

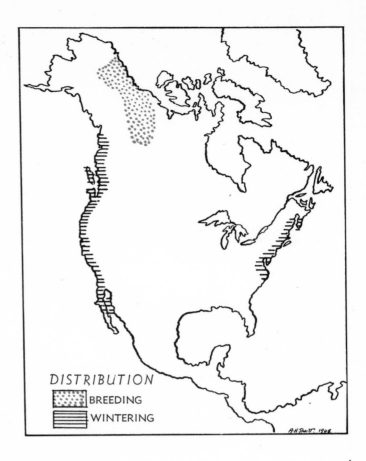

DISTRIBUTION
▓ BREEDING
≡ WINTERING

COURTSHIP AND NESTING

"Several authors (W. L. Dawson, A. Brooks, C. E. Alford) describe chases in which both sexes take part with much splashing, diving and short flights. Several males may display to one female, and all dive when she does; males carry head and neck erect and at intervals dip beak in water, while females also bow (Alford). A. Brooks saw three or four males whirling around female like whirligig beetles; while C. L. Whittle, who observed courtship in October, records males bowing so deeply as to immerse their heads and performing sudden short flights of about 75 feet, raising wings as they alighted till tips nearly touched.

"Little on record as to nesting, and that by earlier workers. Audubon records a nest in a treacherous swamp; R. Macfarlane found a number of nests at some distance from water, well concealed under spreading branches of pine and spruce. Nest is a mere depression in ground, lined with weeds, grasses and down, which is very dark brown, with whitish centers and tips. Eggs: five to seven (also recorded to nine), ovate or elliptical ovate, smooth but not glossy, creamy-white to pinkish-buff." Eggs average 2.42 by 1.69 inches.

FOOD

"According to J. C. Phillips, 90 per cent of the food is animal matter, chiefly marine Mollusca, especially black mussels (*Modiola modiolus*) and northwest oysters (*Ostrea lurida*); but also razor shells (*Siliquaria*), scallops (*Pecten*), *Spisula, Nucula,* etc.; Crustacea (crayfish, crabs, barnacles, water fleas, etc.); Echinodermata (brittle-stars [Ophiurida] and sea cucumbers [Holothuroidea]); Coelenterata (hydroids and sea anenomes) and Annelida (marine worms); also fish spawn. Some insects recorded: Ephemeroptera (nymphs of Ephemeridae), Coleoptera (larva of water beetles), and Diptera. Vegetable matter (10 per cent) includes water celery, buds, pondweeds, *Zostera,* and marine algae."

WEIGHTS

Male—*Average of 10:* 2 pounds, 3 ounces. *Extremes:* 1 pound, 7 ounces to 2 pounds, 8 ounces.

Female—*Average of 7:* 2 pounds. *Extremes:* 1 pound, 8 ounces to 2 pounds, 3 ounces.

MIGRATIONS

"In spring the main northward flight takes place in May, when in countless numbers they wing their way along the coast to their summer breeding grounds. In autumn the return voyage is made in September and October, the older birds usually preceding the younger by a week or two." (Kortright)

REFERENCES

Kortright, Francis H., *The Ducks, Geese and Swans of North America,* 1942.
Witherby, Jourdain, Ticehurst and Tucker, *Handbook of British Birds,* 1943.
The A.O.U. Check-list of North American Birds (Fourth Edition), 1931.

Surf Scoter

WHITE-WINGED SCOTER

(Melanitta fusca deglandi)

MALE   FEMALE

COMMON NAMES

Sea Coot, Bay Coot, Scooter.

DESCRIPTION

A large, black sea duck with conspicuous white speculum. Female is brown with smaller, but still conspicuous, white wing patches.

Adult male in flight. Large, heavy-bodied, all-black sea duck with *conspicuous white wing patches (specula) on trailing edge of wing close to body.* At close range, *a small, comma-shaped white spot enclosing eye (curving upwards and behind)* can be seen. Has a habit of flying along in Indian file close to water, but is seldom seen in large flocks in the interior.

Adult male on water. Large, *all-black duck, with white comma-shaped spot enclosing eye and curving upwards behind.* The white wing patch is partly or completely concealed by the flank feathers when the bird is at rest.

Adult female in flight and on water. Large, dusky-brown duck with *whitish spots before (and under) and behind (and level) with the eye.* These spots separate the female from all other scoters or eiders but are not conspicuous in flight.

DISTRIBUTION

Breeds from northwestern Alaska (and casually Greenland), south to the Gulf of St. Lawrence, James Bay, Mackenzie, the interior of Ungava Peninsula, south-central Manitoba, Saskatchewan and Alberta. Winters on the Atlantic coast from the Bay of Fundy to Florida and on the Pacific from the Aleutian Islands to Lower California; also on the Great Lakes and sparingly in the interior of southern British Columbia, and in Louisiana. Casual in Great Britain, France, Finland, Scandinavia, Belgium, Holland and on Bering Island.

COURTSHIP AND NESTING

Phillips, quoting U.S. Biological Survey notes, describes the male "as lowering neck until it rests on water, then rushing along with rapid strokes of feet to pause near female, throw head erect and call." J. M. Edson's observations, quoted from Bent (1925) via Kortright, suggest pairing ceremonies. He records, "Ten of these birds were bunched together and actively swimming and plunging about within a circle perhaps ten or twelve feet in diameter. . . . At the center of the group two birds would assume a pose as if billing and caressing each other, one with its head elevated, the other's depressed, the bills coming in contact. The pose would last only two or three seconds, until some other bird would approach one of them from behind; then the latter would suddenly turn and chase it away, the pursued bird taking a circular course around the flock. Sometimes both the posing birds would be simultaneously approached, and each would turn upon its assailant." Edson saw this performance for half an hour and it was still going on when he left. The observations were made in December and again in February.

The nest is on the ground, often at a considerable distance from water. A cavity is scraped in the ground and is lined with plant debris and dark gray down from the female's breast. Usually it is well concealed under shrubs or bushes. The eggs are pale salmon or pinkish and are finely granulated or pitted. There are nine to fourteen in a clutch, and they measure 2.57 by 1.80 inches.

FOOD

Kortright states, "The strength and degree of elasticity of the stomach of this sea-fowl is surprising, and the grinding power of its gizzard is almost unbelievable. Oysters and other mollusks are swallowed whole, and many shells that require a hard blow of a hammer to break are readily ground up and chemically disintegrated in the gizzard . . ." Of the total food in 819 stomachs, examined in many parts of the White-winged Scoter's range, in every month except June and September, 94 per cent was animal matter. Mollusks, including rock clams, oysters, blue mussels and scallops, accounted for 75 per cent, the balance being made up of crustaceans, insects, fishes and miscellaneous animal food. The 6 per cent of plant food included eel grass, bur reed and unidentified items.

WEIGHTS

Male—*Average of* 7: 3 pounds, 8 ounces. *Extremes:* 3 pounds to 3 pounds, 15 ounces.

Female—*Average of* 15: 2 pounds, 10 ounces. *Extremes:* 2 pounds, 2 ounces to 3 pounds, 1 ounce.

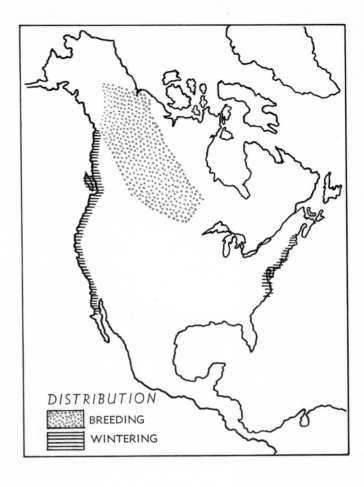

DISTRIBUTION
⬚ BREEDING
≡ WINTERING

SOUTHWARD MIGRATION

Very few White-winged Scoters are shot on the Canadian prairies for very few are seen. They breed chiefly in the intermediate belt between the prairies and the Arctic, except in the Mackenzie Basin and Alaska, where environmental conditions are similar. They appear to move east through the forested belt and west through the high passes of the Rockies to the coasts. We know little of these migrations; but Forbush says their season in Massachusetts is from August 10 to May 25, and W. E. Clyde Todd says that they are the most numerous of the scoters on Lake Erie between October 9 and November 19.

REFERENCES

Bailey, Alfred M., *The Birds of Cape Prince of Wales, Alaska*, 1943.
Forbush, Edward Howe, *Birds of Massachusetts and Other New England States*, 1925.
Kortright, Francis H., *The Ducks, Geese and Swans of North America*, 1942.
Swarth, Harry S., *Birds of Nunivak Island, Alaska*, 1934.
Todd, W. E. Clyde, *Birds of Western Pennsylvania*, 1940.
The A.O.U. Check-list of North American Birds (Fourth Edition), 1931.

White=winged Scoter

SHOVELLER

(Spatula clypeata)

MALE   FEMALE

COMMON NAMES

Spoonbill, Spoony.

DESCRIPTION

A gaudy-colored duck with an oversize spatulate (spoon-shaped) bill which gives it a distinctive appearance on the water or in the air. The metallic green or blue color of the head (depending on the light angle incidence), grotesque bill, white breast and chestnut sides are distinctive of the male. The female is like a female Mallard except for the bill and her habit of riding front end down and rear end high. The feet are orange-red in both sexes and can often be seen as they swim around.

Adult male in flight. Dark head, large bill, white breast, chestnut sides and belly. Chalky-blue patches on fore wings (shoulders) and two diagonal white streaks on back. Whitish tail endings. No other duck like it.

Adult male on water. Bow end down. Heavy bill pointed downward looks out of proportion with rest of design. Glossy green (or blue) head, very lustrous, changes color with different angles of view. White breast, chestnut sides, white flank, black rear end paling to tips of tail feathers.

Adult female in flight. Drab like a Mallard female, but the outsize, heavy-looking bill is distinctive.

Adult female on water. Like a Mallard, but bill looks too big for the bird. Lower mandible is reddish-orange. Rides low in front—higher behind.

DISTRIBUTION

The Shoveller is found almost all over the northern hemisphere and in winter in Africa, South America, Hawaii and Australia. It is one of the most widely distributed of waterfowl. In North America the breeding range is chiefly west of the Great Lakes from Eskimo Point (Hudson Bay), discontinuously through northern Manitoba, the valley of the Saskatchewan River, up the Mackenzie Valley to its delta, and from the Alaska coast region south to New Mexico, Arizona and southern California. Formerly through the Mississippi Valley and the eastern states, where it seems to be making efforts to re-establish itself. Winters from southern British Columbia south on the Pacific side to and including Mexico and Central America, Columbia and the Hawaiian Islands; the southern interior states; the Atlantic coast from South Carolina southward and the West Indies.

NORTHWARD MIGRATION

Arrives in Canada about the middle of April and reaches peak numbers about the end of the month. They may be seen throughout the month of May wherever there is a ditch or puddle of water—mating, selecting territory and loafing.

COURTSHIP AND NESTING

The courtship flight of the Shoveller is as spectacular as that of any species. They are as energetic as the Teals in that respect. Hochbaum records seeing eighteen males in pursuit of a single female late in the season. I have seen four to seven males darting and evoluting after one female with all the vim and vigor of blackbirds in the mating season. The idea that Shovellers are polyandrous is erroneous, in my opinion. Kortright says they are, but my observations would indicate that mated pairs will tolerate sexually non-active males only as novices or hangers-on. Sexually active males are as keen rivals as those of any other species. The fiercest fight I ever saw among waterfowl was between two rival Shoveller males. They approached each other with heads bobbing like pistons and then tore into each other like bantams. They were on and over each other just like bantams and made the feathers fly. The flights all have the verve and speed of Teals, with the same bewildering changes of height and direction and with the queerest peeps, whistles and squeaky quacks that one may hear.

FOOD

The Shoveller is adept at catching insects. The specialized bill, however, is designed to sift mud and water, through the sieve that adorns the edges of the mandibles, and trap the edible material. They seldom tip up or dive. They also feed on aquatic vegetation, but 35 per cent of their food is animal matter.

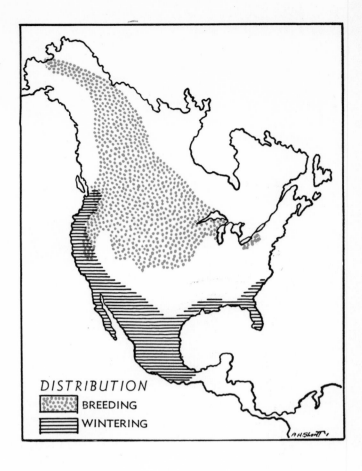

DISTRIBUTION
BREEDING
WINTERING

WEIGHTS

The weight of Shovellers is less than their appearance would lead one to believe.

Male—*Average of 86:* 1 pound, 3 ounces.
Female—*Average of 68:* 1 pound, 4 ounces.

SOUTHWARD MIGRATION

Contrary to current literature, considerable numbers of Shovellers stay in the West until driven out by the first storms of winter. The bulk of the migration is in September and October.

REFERENCES

Hochbaum, H. Albert, *The Canvasback on a Prairie Marsh,* 1944.
Kortright, Francis H., *The Ducks, Geese and Swans of North America,* 1942.
Mair and Macfarlane, *Through the Mackenzie Basin,* 1908.
The A.O.U. Check-list of North American Birds (Fourth Edition), 1931.

Shoveller

BLUE-WINGED TEAL

(Anas discors)

FEMALE   MALE

COMMON NAME

Blue-wing.

DESCRIPTION

A small, swift, surface-feeding duck with pale blue patches on the fore-wing (shoulder), from which the species gets its name. Has increased considerably during last five years.

Adult male and female in flight. Small size; rapid wing beats; swift. Large pale blue patches on fore-wing—not so prominent in female or juvenile as adult male. These patches appear white under certain light conditions. Small size will separate from Shoveller and Baldpate with similarly placed wing patches.

Adult male on water. Small size. General appearance dark gray. Vertical white crescent in front of eye. Undertail coverts dark with a prominent white spot on the flank.

Adult female on water. Small size. Lack of any distinguishing marks except when she spreads a wing and reveals the blue patch,

which otherwise is concealed. Difficult to tell apart from the female Green-winged Teal except by the blue wing patch. Indistinguishable in the field from the female Cinnamon Teal, which also has the blue wing patch. The latter is rare within the breeding range of the Blue-wing, hence chances of confusion are rare. On the water these females are usually found in company with their easily identified mates, and that is a convincing identification.

NORTHWARD MIGRATION

Average date of arrival in southern Minnesota, about March 21; northern Minnesota, about April 13; southern Manitoba, about April 24. Usually a few days earlier than April 24 in southern Saskatchewan and Alberta. Peak of migration in Manitoba first week in May. Blue-wings are among the last of the duck species to arrive—only Ruddy Ducks and White-winged Scoters being later. Blue-wings follow well behind the retreating snow-line. They reach the breeding grounds when the danger of a vicious backlash of winter is remote.

Normal flying speeds are from 35 to 45 miles per hour, in rela-tion to the ground—varying to higher speeds in accordance with strength of tailwinds, or in short bursts under pressure of fear. Small size and rapid wing beats create an illusion of super-speed.

COURTSHIP AND NESTING

Pairing takes place during the winter. Most of the birds are in pairs on their arrival in Canada. This, however, does not inhibit the courtship displays, which are as exciting and spectacular as those of any other species.

Unmated or amorous males pay attention to mated females and keep the rightful mate in a constant dither. He drives away intrud-ers with a great show of fury, but combats are not of a serious nature. The female sometimes aids her mate in ejecting a suitor from their pre-empted water territory. Head-bobbing is a standard display of sexually active birds, and wild flights with two or more males in pursuit of a single female are common sights in May. Hoch-baum records seeing as many as twenty-four males in pursuit of one female in early June, when unmated females would be scarce. Nesting is usually within one hundred feet of water but may be as far away as one mile. In Manitoba, where small poplar bluffs abound around marshes, there is usually a depression in the middle of a bluff in which water lies from the melting snows, for a longer period than exposed pools on the open prairies. The Blue-wing nests close to the prairie pool and spends the off-nest period with her male in the nearby secluded pool of the poplar bluff—an en-vironment niche shared by no other duck species in my experience.

Blue-wings increased remarkably during the 1938–43 period and held their own in 1944–45. The nest is a neat cup-shaped de-pression in the ground, under cover of prairie grass or wolfberry (*Symphoricarpus occidentalis*) or any other available cover; lined with grass and walled around with down (light brownish-gray and white) from the female's breast, which she spreads over the eggs to conceal them and keep them warm when she leaves.

FOOD

About 70 per cent of the food of the Blue-wing—taken the year around—is vegetable matter, the balance being composed largely of aquatic insects, mollusks and crustaceans. In the interior its feeding habits are such as to impart a delectable flavor to its flesh.

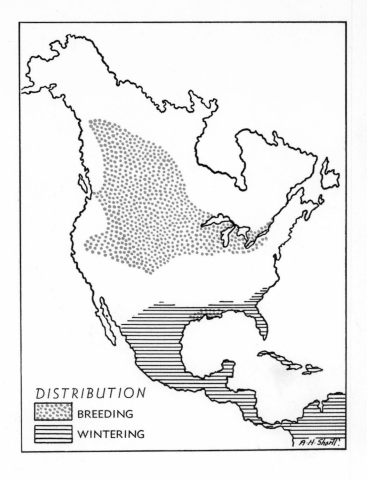

DISTRIBUTION
BREEDING
WINTERING

WEIGHTS

Male—*Average of* 73 : 14.6 ounces.
Female—*Average of* 82 : 13.6 ounces.

SOUTHWARD MIGRATION

Blue-wings start south in August. By the middle of September a majority have departed. Relatively few remain when the hunting season opens in Canada (September 7–29), but a scattering of laggards may be encountered throughout October and odd ones until freeze-up in November. The passage through the United States is also ahead of the hunting seasons for the most part. The species is not so heavily shot as the later migrants.

REFERENCES

Bennett, Logan J., *The Blue-winged Teal*, 1938.
Hochbaum, H. Albert, *The Canvasback on a Prairie Marsh*, 1944.
Kortright, Francis H., *The Ducks, Geese and Swans of North America*, 1942.
The A.O.U. Check-list of North American Birds (Fourth Edition), 1931.

A.H.Shortt. 1946.

Blue=winged Teal

CINNAMON TEAL

(Anas cyanoptera)

MALE   FEMALE

DESCRIPTION

A strikingly handsome duck of the surface-feeding group. General appearance is cinnamon-red, darker on back, with pale blue wing patches on the fore-wing, in the male.

Adult male in flight. Unlike any other duck in North America. Its cinnamon-red general coloration and blue wing patches are as conspicuous as a neon sign. Small size and rapid wing beats are characteristic of all teals.

Adult male on water. Cinnamon-red of head, neck and body—darker on back—leaves no doubt as to identity.

Adult female in flight and on water. Cannot be distinguished in the field from female Blue-winged Teal. Best identification is to see her in company with her unmistakable mate. The bill is longer and heavier than that of the Blue-wing.

NORTHWARD MIGRATION

Spring migration takes place in March and April. The center of abundance of this species is west of the Rocky Mountains—the only North American duck species about which this can be said—and, since breeding and wintering ranges overlap, the extent of migration of some individuals may be quite short. It is probable, however, that the birds which go farthest north are those which winter farthest south.

DISTRIBUTION

The wintering range is from the southwestern United States south through western Mexico to Panama. The breeding range extends from southern British Columbia into Saskatchewan and Alberta (rarely), Montana, Washington, Oregon, California, Wyoming, Kansas, and states intervening; south to northern Mexico and Lower California.

An entirely separate group of Cinnamon Teals occurs in South America from Buenos Aires and the Peruvian Andes to the Falkland Islands and the Straits of Magellan; also from Brazil, Paraguay, Bolivia and Peru (rarely Ecuador and Colombia) to central Patagonia and Chiloe Island. This is the only case of the same species of duck with disconnected ranges in the two hemispheres.

COURTSHIP AND NESTING

The courtship display is accompanied by much splashing and rushing by rival males at each other around the seemingly indifferent object of their attentions. The head-bobbing response of sexually active birds is provocative, but combats are devoid of viciousness and nobody gets hurt. After the female has made her choice, she helps her mate to drive away disappointed suitors. The males are said to be joyously playful among themselves, indulging in a game of leap-frog—"one will rush at the other, leap over him and alight on the water just ahead; the hindmost will take his turn at the leap and so on."

The nest is placed in a variety of situations, from over water among reeds—a neat, basket-like structure—to a shallow depression in the ground scantily lined with weeds or debris and with no pretense at concealment. The eggs are white or pinkish, usually ten or twelve in number, and measure 1.87 by 1.36 inches.

When the female leads her ducklings on the water, the male often attends them and shows even more concern that she when danger threatens. This is unusual among ducks. The only other species which frequently does the same is the Ruddy Duck. Occasionally the male Pintail will join the family party.

FOOD

Sedges, pondweeds, grasses and smartweeds are preferred foods in the diet, which is 80 per cent vegetable matter. The balance is chiefly insects.

WEIGHTS

Male—*Average of 13 : 12 ounces.*
Female—*Average of 11 : 12.5 ounces.*

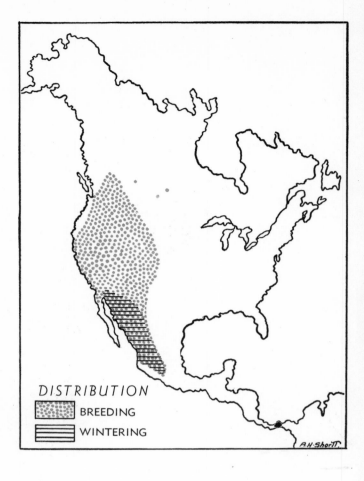

DISTRIBUTION
▒▒▒ BREEDING
≡≡≡ WINTERING

SOUTHWARD MIGRATION

Southward migration takes place in September and October and consists of relatively short hops from north to south portions of a continuous breeding and wintering range.

REFERENCES

Kortright, Francis H., *The Ducks, Geese and Swans of North America*, 1942.
The A.O.U. Check-list of North American Birds (Fourth Edition), 1931.

Cinnamon Teal

GREEN-WINGED TEAL

(Anas carolinense)

MALE   FEMALE

COMMON NAMES

Green-wing, Common Teal.

DESCRIPTION

One of the smallest, speediest and daintiest of the surface-feeding ducks.

Adult male in flight. Small size, rapid wing beats, speedy flight are features of all teals. At ordinary observing distances, the male shows no distinguishing field marks, which is, in itself, the best identifying feature. Under favorable light conditions, the "green flash" of the wing patch (speculum) may be seen.

Adult male on water. Small size. *Narrow, vertical white crescent in front of folded wing,* and *conspicuous yellow-ochre colored spot on the flank* (undertail coverts) are distinctive. This spot varies in color to almost white. At ordinary observing distances field glasses

are needed to bring out colors of chestnut head—glossy green patch on sides of head.

Adult female in flight. Small size, rapid wing beats, swift flight and *absolute lack of any distinctive markings* is diagnostic. Brownish (drab) bird with white lower breast and belly. Green flash of speculum may be seen under favorable light conditions.

Adult female on water. Small size, no distinctive markings. Easily confused with females of Blue-winged and Cinnamon teals. The best identification is to see her in company with her mate.

DISTRIBUTION

Breeds in Newfoundland and across the continent from the northern tier of states north to the limit of trees. Nesting range extends southward in the mountainous regions to northern New Mexico. Winters from southern British Columbia and Nova Scotia south through the United States, wherever open water can be found, to the West Indies, Mexico and Central American republics.

NORTHWARD MIGRATION

Arrives in southern Canada early in April—peak of migration about April 18. The first arrivals are paired birds. A majority pass on to nest in more northerly areas. Comparatively few remain to nest in the sloughs and marshes of southern Manitoba or Saskatchewan, but they become progressively more numerous as you go west into south-central Saskatchewan and Alberta. The main breeding grounds are north of the treeless prairies.

The small size, rapid wing beats and sizzling flight of teals have led to some fantastic guesses on their speeds. They are credited with 100 miles per hour in relation to the ground. The writer has never seen convincing evidence of this. With strong enough tailwinds it might be possible; but, after considerable experience observing waterfowl from airplanes, I am sure that, even under pressure, any species of duck can easily be overhauled by a plane traveling 95 miles per hour air speed. I believe the Canvasback is faster at normal migrating speeds than any of the teals.

COURTSHIP AND NESTING

Very little has been recorded about the courtship of the Greenwing. I have never witnessed the display. Numerous authors refer to Bent's (1923) account of George M. Sutton's description of two males swimming around a single female in perfect harmony of movement, about two feet apart, with bills pointed slightly upward and their heads drawn back in a stiff, uncomfortable-looking manner. The female took no notice of the two swimming at "tantalizingly deliberate speed" as they circled around her at a distance of about six feet. Finally she made a rush at one, "whereupon he stood up in the water, lifted his wings slightly, and with rapidly churning feet made a most unusual noise—like a fine jet of water impinging on some object." The other male repeated the antic and sometimes both did it together.

The nest is a neat cavity lined with grasses, well concealed in vegetation, around sloughs, ponds, along river banks and muskegs; usually close to water but sometimes at considerable distances away at the base of willows or other shrubs. Copious down is added to the nest as incubation proceeds and is used to cover eight to fifteen eggs, which constitute a full clutch. Eggs vary in color from pure white to cream or buffy-olive and average 1.80 by 1.35 inches. Incubation period is 21–23 days by female only.

Over a period of six years, Ducks Unlimited's keemen have recorded 11,071 females with 78,210 young, which gives an average brood of 7.64 in the last week of July. The general duck brood average is six, so this species has unusual nesting success.

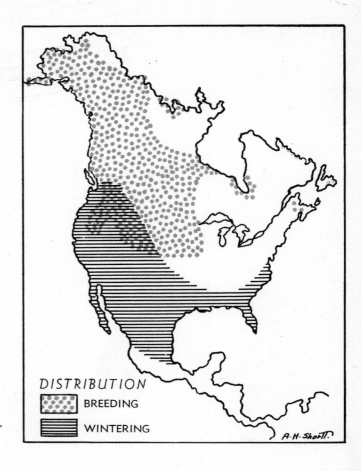

DISTRIBUTION

▨ BREEDING

▤ WINTERING

A. H. Shortt.

FOOD

Ninety per cent of the Green-wing's food is vegetable matter, but on the Pacific coast many of them feed on rotting salmon, which spoils their flesh for the table. In the interior, where they are restricted to sedges, pondweeds, grasses and other fine duck foods, they are regarded as "tops" for flavor.

WEIGHTS

Male—*Average of 130:* 12.8 ounces. *Extremes:* 12 to 14 ounces.
Female—*Average of 68:* 12 ounces. *Extremes:* 9 to 13 ounces.

SOUTHWARD MIGRATION

In late September or early October, Green-wings gather in spectacular concentrations in favorite marshes, where they may be seen swarming like blackbirds. The third week in October witnesses a general exodus, and by the end of the month nearly all are gone.

Green=winged Teal

A.H.Shortt. 1946

WOOD DUCK

(Aix sponsa)

MALE   FEMALE

COMMON NAMES

Summer Duck, Wood Duck.

DESCRIPTION

The male is regarded as one of the world's most beautiful water-fowl. Elongated crest (never raised) is worn by both sexes.

Adult male in flight. Medium size; white breast and belly; white throat and two white bars which extend upward, one toward the eye and the other ending in the black of the hind neck. Chestnut sides of body dark. Dark tail is long for a duck and wedge-shaped— a good field mark. Head is carried above the level of the body, bill pointed down.

Adult male on water. Gorgeous colors, crested head with its conspicuous up-pointed white bars. Black and white crescents in front of wing, and proud carriage, are distinctive.

Adult female in flight. Medium size; swift, direct flight; white breast and belly. Long, wedge-shaped tail. Carries head and bill like male.

Adult female on water. A drab, gray-brown duck with brown elongated crest. A white spot encloses the eye and tapers off to a point behind the eye.

NORTHWARD MIGRATION

Wood Ducks return to the northern part of their range in March or early April. Over much of their range the breeding and wintering grounds are continuous, so that migratory movements are not well defined.

DISTRIBUTION

Breeds from Nova Scotia and New Brunswick west to Manitoba and southern British Columbia. Summer resident locally in nearly every state in the Union. Winters from southern British Columbia, central Missouri, southern Illinois and southern Virginia south to Jamaica and central Mexico. Rarely north to Michigan and Massachusetts. Casual in Bermuda.

113

COURTSHIP AND NESTING

The favorite haunts of the Wood Duck are secluded ponds in the woods or tree-bordered streams where moss-grown deadfalls slant into the water, making convenient perches on which the birds can bask in the sun and preen their lovely plumage. They are quite garrulous among themselves, and a courting party's antics are punctuated by guttural notes from the males and musical squeaks and whistles from both sexes. Rival males make a pretense at fighting, but beyond a dislodged feather or two the combats are not serious. The male swims around the object of his affection with puffed-out throat, arched neck and agitated crest. He bows and displays his fine feathers to best advantage. She makes her choice and touches him with her bill in caressing manner and then joins him in repelling intruders of either sex.

In due course they fly off into the woods to the nesting site—usually a pileated woodpecker's old hole or a natural cavity in a live or dead tree. Nesting boxes are favored and have been used with great success in the Illinois River bottoms by members of the U.S. Fish and Wildlife Service and Illinois Natural History Survey. The female can squeeze through an aperture no larger than four inches in diameter. It is amazing to watch the headlong flight of the female into the nesting entrance. With scarcely a check in her swift flight she dashes in with reckless disregard for a possible broken neck.

Logging and the cutting of dead trees by settlers has reduced nesting sites. The Wood Duck's chief home-builder—the pileated woodpecker—has retreated before civilization, thus upsetting one of nature's fine inter-relationships. The species has shown a gratifying increase in the last few years, particularly in Michigan, Illinois and southern British Columbia.

Twelve to fifteen dull white or creamy white eggs are laid.

FOOD

Ninety per cent of the food is vegetable matter—duck weeds, cypress cones and galls, sedges and tubers, grasses and grass seeds, pondweeds, acorns and beechnuts, water lily seeds and leaves of water shield; smartweeds, docks, bur reed, coontail, wild celery and other available aquatic and terrestrial plants and seeds. Dragon and damsel flies and nymphs, bugs, beetles, grasshoppers, crickets, flies, wasps and spiders make up the bulk of the 10 per cent animal matter consumed.

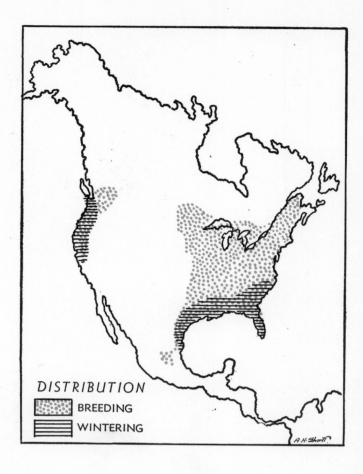

DISTRIBUTION
:::: BREEDING
≡≡≡ WINTERING

WEIGHTS

Male—*Average of 30 :* 1 pound, 8 ounces.
Female—*Average of 13 :* 1 pound, 2½ ounces.

SOUTHWARD MIGRATION

Leaves Canada and the northern tier of states in September and October. Elsewhere it is found both in summer and winter.

REFERENCES

Forbush, Edward Howe, *Birds of Massachusetts and Other New England States* (3 volumes), 1925.
Kortright, Francis H., *The Ducks, Geese and Swans of North America*, 1942.
Roberts, Thomas S., *Birds of Minnesota*, 1932.
The A.O.U. Check-list of North American Birds (Fourth Edition), 1931.

Wood Duck

BLUE GOOSE

(Chen caerulescens)

COMMON NAMES

Blue Wavy, Kung-o-vik (Eskimo).

DESCRIPTION

A medium-sized dusky goose with *white head and neck* and variable amounts of white on the underparts. Gets its name from bluish-white wing coverts—not conspicuous in the field.

Male and female on water. A dark, medium-sized goose with *white head and neck.* Almost always associated with Lesser Snow Geese on land and water, on the breeding grounds, on migration and on the wintering grounds.

Male and female in flight. The dusky body and wings, contrasting with the white head and neck, makes identification easy.

DISTRIBUTION

Breeds on Baffin Island in the Bowman Bay region of Foxe Basin, on southwest Southampton Island, in the Perry River District, Queen Maud Gulf, Arctic Canada, the vicinity of Eskimo Point and the west coast of Hudson Bay. The principal known breeding grounds, discovered by J. Dewey Soper in 1929, are on Baffin Island. Winters on the coastal marshes of Louisiana, near the mouth of the Mississippi west—in decreasing numbers—to eastern Texas.

NORTHWARD MIGRATION

Leaves Louisiana during the last ten days of March and pauses, while winter retreats, in Iowa, Nebraska, South and North Dakota, Minnesota, Manitoba and on both coasts of Hudson Bay, where they feed on the tide flats for about three weeks. Associated always with Lesser Snow Geese, one branch follows the west coast to the vicinity of Rankin Inlet and over to Southampton Island. The main flight follows the east coast across Hudson Strait to Baffin Island. During the past two years there have been reports of increasing numbers of Blue Geese migrating with Snows through southern Alberta.

COURTSHIP AND NESTING

Just before migration starts from Louisiana, the Blue Geese gather into two or three great bands. "During these gatherings," states McIlhenny, "the unmated birds select their mates. This causes conflicts among the males and they fight hard and long, using the beak to hold an opponent, and both wings to beat him." Like most, if not all geese, mating is for life.

On the Baffin Island breeding grounds the birds are concentrated on a comparatively narrow strip of marshy land bounded by mud flats. The nests are built on top of slight ridges on the tundra, on fairly dry ground. Most nests are made of shredded moss lined with dead grasses and pale down—others entirely of grass and a species of chickweed. Three to five white or creamy-white eggs are laid. They average 3.16 by 2.01 inches. Incubation period is 23–25 days.

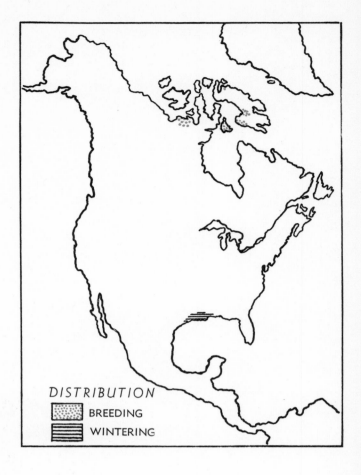

DISTRIBUTION

▨ BREEDING

▤ WINTERING

FOOD

On the Louisiana marshes Blue Geese feed on seeds of sprangle-top (*Leptochloa fasicularis*), wild millet (*Echinochloa crusgalli*), the root stocks of common three-square bulrush (*Scirpus americanus*), the saltmarsh bulrush (*S. robustus*), cord grass (*Spartina patens*) and the delta duck potato (*Sagittaria platyphylla*). On the tundra, Soper states, "their chief food, for which they grub deep in the soil, appears to be the common tundra grass." During migration on the prairies, the birds work over the cultivated fields gleaning waste grain from the previous year's harvest and consuming the tender new shoots of grasses and weeds.

SOUTHWARD MIGRATION

Leaves the breeding grounds early in September and concentrates on the tide marshes of James and Hannah Bays at the south end of Hudson Bay. There they pause until forced out by the onset of winter. The flight south is over the Great Lakes direct to Louisiana, unless forced down in intervening states by weather conditions. In 1947, on October 25–29, during misty weather, considerable numbers of Blue Geese were shot in Iowa—where previously they had been known only as spring migrants. The departures from normal movements manifest during the past five years indicate that an expansion of range is underway.

WEIGHTS

Male—*Average of 18:* 5 pounds, 5 ounces. *Extremes:* 4 pounds, 7 ounces to 6 pounds, 4 ounces.

Female—*Average of 17:* 4 pounds, 14 ounces. *Extremes:* 4 pounds, 4 ounces to 6 pounds, 4 ounces.

REFERENCES

Kortright, Francis H., *The Ducks, Geese and Swans of North America*, 1942.

Martin, A. C., and Uhler, F. M., "Food of Game Ducks in the United States and Canada," *U.S. Department of Agriculture Technical Bulletin 634*, March, 1939.

McIlhenny, E. A., "The Blue Goose in Its Winter Home," *The Auk*, Volume 49, Number 3 (July, 1932).

Soper, J. Dewey, "The Blue Goose," Northwest Territories and Yukon Branch, Department of the Interior, Ottawa, 1930.

——, "Supplementary Data Concerning the Blue Goose," *Canadian Field National*, Volume 6, Number 5 (September-October, 1946).

Blue Goose

BRANT

(Branta bernicla hrota)

BLACK BRANT

(B. b. nigricans)

THE AMERICAN AND BLACK BRANT ARE ALMOST IDENTICAL ON WATER

COMMON NAME

Brant.

DESCRIPTION

Small, dark geese found almost exclusively on salt water. The Brant, referred to in textbooks as "American" or "Common," has recently lost its subspecific distinction and is now regarded as indistinguishable from the Pale-breasted Brent goose of the Old World. The Black Brant retains its subspecific status, the type species being the Dark-breasted Brent goose.

Male and female on water. Small size (hardly larger than a Mallard); short, black head and neck; dark back sharply contrasting with whitish sides. *Tail uptilted, showing white undertail coverts.* Rides buoyantly like a gull and is graceful in all its movements. Remarks apply to both varieties, except that the Black Brant is darker on the sides.

Male and female in flight. The short, black neck and chest contrast sharply with the white breast in the Pale-breasted form. The black of the chest shades off gradually into slaty-brown of breast and into white of belly in the Black Brant. A white "vee" over the tail is conspicuous in both forms. The flight is swift, wing beats rapid, wings long and pointed and the birds usually fly in long, straggly lines close to water but with frequent changes in elevation. On migration, however, they fly at higher altitudes and sometimes in "vee" formation.

DISTRIBUTION

The Brant breeds in the Arctic regions from Queen Maud gulf, the Canadian Arctic archipelago, northern Ellesmere and Axel Heiberg Islands, both coasts of Greenland, Spitzbergen and (probably) Franz Josef Land. Winters on the Atlantic coast from New Jersey to North Carolina, less frequently to Massachusetts and Florida, and on the Pacific coast of the United States and British Columbia. In Europe to the English Channel, Holland, Germany and Denmark.

The Black Brant breeds on the Arctic coasts and islands from Siberia to Queen Maud Gulf in the Canadian Arctic, where it overlaps with the Pale-breasted form. Winters mainly on the Pacific coast from Vancouver to Lower California and on the Asiatic side to China and Japan. Accidental on the Atlantic coast and Hawaiian Islands. The main northward migration along the Atlantic coast is in March and April. Black Brant migrate similarly, and by May 1 all have departed from the British Columbia coast.

COURTSHIP AND NESTING

Pursuit flights take place on the breeding grounds. The gander and goose are said to spiral up to great heights. The sheer beauty of their movements on water and in the air captivates observers. Brant nest on islands in colonies. The nest is a depression among rocks, lined with moss and copiously walled around with dark down, with which the eggs are covered when the female is away. Incubation is by female only with the gander standing guard. The nests are from three feet to fifty yards apart. The eggs are usually five but vary from four to eight. They are white, but both eggs and down of the Black Brant are darker. They measure 2.65 to 2.87 by 1.75 to 1.95 inches. The nests of the Black Brant are in marshes and on the adjoining tundra and are farther apart—200 to 300 yards. After the nesting season they gather in flocks on sandy flats, but the paler form rafts along the rocky coast among the islands. The peak of the flightless period of molting adults is about July 10.

FOOD

Kortright states, "On their Arctic breeding grounds the food of these birds consists of grass, algae, moss and stalks and leaves of Arctic plants. On the wintering range the preferred food is eel grass (*Zostera*). A blight destroyed eel grass over a large part of its Atlantic coast range some years ago. The U.S. Fish and Wildlife Service, in cooperation with the Wildlife Management Institute, Ducks Unlimited and several state game commissions, is now engaged in a transplanting program to speed its re-establishment. Brant are considered the finest table birds of all geese."

WEIGHTS

Male—*Average of 21 Black Brant:* 3 pounds, 2 ounces. *Extremes:* 2 pounds, 11 ounces to 3 pounds, 11 ounces.

Female—*Average of 3 Brant:* 2 pounds, 6 ounces. *Extremes:* 2 pounds, 3 ounces to 2 pounds, 11 ounces.

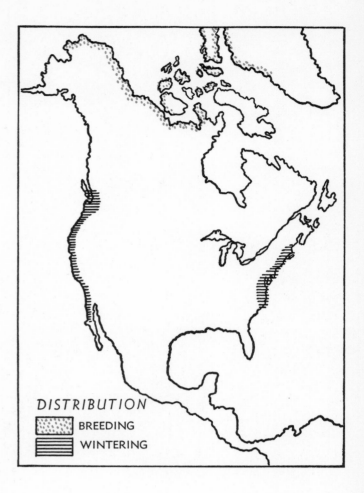

DISTRIBUTION
▦ BREEDING
▤ WINTERING

SOUTHWARD MIGRATION

Leaves the Arctic coast about September 1. The Pale-breasted subspecies travels down the west coast of Hudson Bay into James Bay and east across the Labrador peninsula to the St. Lawrence River and Gulf; thence across Prince Edward Island and the neck of Nova Scotia peninsula to Cape Cod, Nantucket and Long Island to Virginia and North Carolina. The Black Brant migrates down the Pacific coasts of North America and Asia to California and Japan, during the last half of September and first half of October—to reach the California coast in October–November.

REFERENCES

Brandt, Herbert, *Alaska Bird Trails*, 1943.
Forbush, Edward Howe, *Birds of Massachusetts and Other New England States*, 1925.
Gavin, Angus, "Birds of Perry River District, Queen Maud Gulf and Arctic Canada," unpublished manuscript, 1943.
Kortright, Francis H., *The Ducks, Geese and Swans of North America*, 1942.
Witherby, Jourdain, Ticehurst and Tucker, *Handbook of British Birds*, 1943.
The A.O.U. Check-list of North American Birds (Fourth Edition), 1931.
——— (19th Supplement), *The Auk*, Volume 61 (1944), page 443.

Brant

UPPER PAIR—*Black-breasted Brant*
LOWER PAIR—*American Brant*

CANADA GOOSE

(B. canadensis)

COMMON NAMES

Honker—applied to Eastern (Common), Ungava, Great Basin and Western (Pacific) Canada Geese. Little Honker—applied to Lesser and Athabasca Canada Geese.

DESCRIPTION

Adult male and female in flight. Large size; slow, measured wing beats. Dark body; black neck and head, with prominent white patch under chin and extending up sides of head to behind eye. Black tail and rump separated by a white bar, which is conspicuous when birds take off and are going away.

Adult male and female on water. Large size, gray-brown body, black neck and head and conspicuous white cheek patches render identification easy.

DISTRIBUTION

In recent years Canada Geese have been the subject of considerable study by taxonomists. The latest revision is that of John W. Aldrich, "Speciation in the White-Cheeked Geese," *Wilson Bulletin*, Volume 58, Number 2 (June, 1946), pages 94–103. The small Cackling Geese are proposed as full species—*B. hutchinsi*—and three subspecies are recognized. Here we confine ourselves to the *canadensis* group as follows:

Eastern (Common) Canada Goose. (*B. c. canadensis*). Breeds in the Maritime region of Quebec, Labrador and Newfoundland; winters from Nova Scotia south to Florida.

Ungava Canada Goose. (*B. c. interior*). "Breeds on the east coast of Hudson and James Bays; in migration to southern United States, mainly west of the Appalachian Mountains."

Great Basin Canada Goose. (*B. c. moffitti*). Geographic distribution. "Eastern Washington and northeastern North Dakota to northeastern California and central Nebraska. The breeding Canada Geese of southern Alberta and Saskatchewan are probably of this subspecies.

Pacific (formerly White-cheeked, later Western) Canada Goose. (*B. c. occidentalis*). Ranges from the Queen Charlotte Islands, British Columbia, and along the coast of southeastern Alaska to the vicinity of Prince William Sound.

These four are the largest forms of Canada Geese, averaging

nine pounds or more in weight. The next two subspecies are smaller
—averaging between five and six pounds. They are the Lesser Canada (Hutchin's) Goose (*B. c. leucopareia*) and the Athabasca Canada Goose (*B. c. parvipes*). The Lesser breeds from the islands of
northeastern Asia east to Baffin Island and winters from northern
Washington to northern Mexico. The Athabasca Canada Goose
breeds—so far as at present known—in the northern portions of the
Prairie Provinces of Canada and winters as far south as Vera Cruz,
Mexico.

COURTSHIP AND NESTING

The Canada Goose mates for life, and it is said that, should one
be killed, the survivor remains widowed for the balance of life. (This
is a belief rather than an established scientific fact. In captivity
widower ganders have been known to mate again, but whether this
occurs in the wild is unknown.) Audubon (1840)—quoted by Kortright—gives a graphic description of the courtship of Canada Geese.
As is to be expected in such long-term commitments, fierce battles
rage between rivals for a female, and victory goes to the most vig-
orous combatant. The victor "advances gallantly toward the object
of contention, his head raised scarcely an inch from the ground, his
bill open to its full stretch, his fleshy tongue elevated, his eyes darting
fiery glances; and as he moves he hisses loudly, while the emotion he
experiences causes his quills to shake and his feathers to rustle. Now
he is close to her, who in his eyes is all loveliness, his neck bending
gracefully in all directions, passing all around her and occasionally
touching her body. As she congratulates him on his victory and
acknowledges his affection, they move their heads in a hundred
curious ways.

"The Canada Goose usually nests on the ground near water,
the type of nest varying with the locality. Generally the nest is a
depression in the ground lined with material from the vicinity: sticks,
flags or grasses, and soft gray down. Sometimes the nests are large,
bulky affairs of about two feet in outside diameter; and again they
may be mere depressions with scanty linings of any sort. In certain
parts of the country nests will occasionally be found in trees, and
in such instances are often the disused nests of ospreys, hawks or
other large birds. The number of eggs varies from four to ten, but
the usual set consists of five or six. The eggs, when freshly laid, are
of a creamy-white color and the average size is 3.37 by 2.29 inches.
The period of incubation is 28 to 30 days and is performed by the
goose alone. While the gander never sits on the eggs, he is always in
attendance ready to protect the family from any danger."

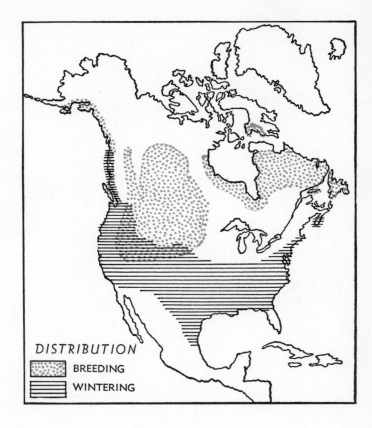

DISTRIBUTION
- ⠂⠂⠂ BREEDING
- ≡≡≡ WINTERING

WEIGHTS

The Eastern (Common), Great Basin and Pacific (Western),
undifferentiated as to age and sex, are said to average heavier—9
pounds or over—than Elder's average for the Ungava Canada Goose,
which is given below. The Lesser and Athabasca Canada Geese
weigh between 5 and 6 pounds. Elder derived the following figures
from a study of 1,028 live *B. c. interior*:

Male—*Adult average*: 8 pounds, 4 ounces. *Heaviest*: 11 pounds, 9
ounces. *Juvenile average*: 7 pounds, 5 ounces.

Female—*Adult average*: 7 pounds. *Juvenile average*: 6 pounds, 5
ounces.

REFERENCES

Aldrich, John W., "Speciation in the White-cheeked Geese," *Wilson Bulletin*, Volume
    58, Number 2 (1946), pages 94-103.
Elder, William H., "Age and Sex Criteria and Weights of Canada Geese," *Journal of
    Wildlife Management*, Volume 10, Number 2 (1946), pages 93-111.
Kortright, Francis H., *The Ducks, Geese and Swans of North America*, 1942.
Todd, W. E. Clyde, "A New Eastern Race of the Canada Goose," *The Auk*, Volume
    55, Number 4 (1938), pages 661-662.
The A.O.U. Check-list of North American Birds (Fourth Edition), 1931.
———— (20th Supplement), *The Auk*, Volume 62, Number 3 (1945).
———— (22nd Supplement), *The Auk*, Volume 64, Number 3 (1947).

Canada Goose

EMPEROR GOOSE

(Philacte canagica)

COMMON NAMES

Japanese Goose, Not-cha-flick (Eskimo).

DESCRIPTION

Sexes alike. A medium-sized goose with ashy-blue plumage margined with black and white bars. A strikingly beautiful bird.

Male and female on water. Medium size; stocky build; ashy, blue-gray body; white head and hindneck, usually stained with rust; black chin, throat and foreneck. The sharp contrast between black foreneck and white hindneck is distinctive.

Male and female in flight. Medium size, chunky outline. All-gray body with white head and tail. Flight is swift and usually in line abreast. Rapid wing beats. Orange-yellow feet. Juveniles are similar to adults, except heads are dusky.

DISTRIBUTION

Breeds on the northwest coast of Alaska from the mouth of the Kuskokwim River to the north side of the Seward Peninsula, Point

Barrow, St. Lawrence Island, and the coast of Siberia from East Cape to Koliuchin Bay. Winters mainly in the Aleutian Islands and along the Alaskan Peninsula, as far east as Bristol Bay and west to the Commander Islands, straggling to central British Columbia, Washington, Oregon, California and the Hawaiian Islands.

NORTHWARD MIGRATION

The northward migration is long and drawn out. Brandt records the first migrant in the Hooper Bay region, Alaska, on May 15; but the real flight did not begin until May 23. From then on for more than a month, flock after flock hurried north, with only an occasional lull. Further north, at Cape Prince of Wales, Bailey (1922) saw the first migrants on May 19, and they became common from May 29 on.

COURTSHIP AND NESTING

Brandt (1920) was of the opinion that Emperor Geese were mated when they arrived on the breeding grounds at Igiak Bay. Nelson (1913) reported, "Almost at once after their arrival," they appeared to be mated, the males walking around the females, swinging their heads and uttering low love notes. The males are extremely jealous and pugnacious and drive away any of their own or other species that approach too close. Emperor Geese nest along the sea-coast among the driftwood or on islands and points of the larger marshy lakes back from the coast a few miles. The nest is a hollow in the ground lined with grasses and increasing amounts of pale, smoky-gray down, which, possibly, is contributed from the breasts of both sexes. It is not definitely known whether or not both sexes share incubation duties, but the males do not stand on guard with the same close attention as the Canada or White-fronted Geese, although they are not far away. Four to eight creamy-white eggs are laid but they soon become nest-stained. Incubation starts when the set is complete and lasts for 24 days. The eggs measure 3.09 by 2.05 inches (average). The nesting period is also long and drawn out and fresh eggs may be found from June 2 to July 10, the later nests probably being second attempts. Newly-hatched young are very trusting and will climb all over a human intruder without any sign of fear.

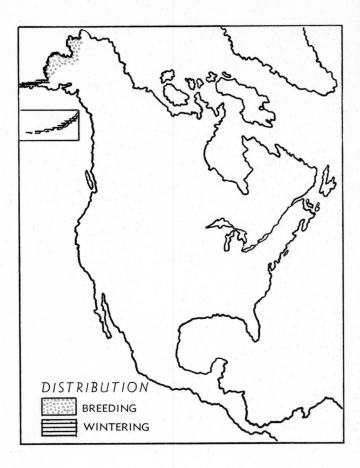

DISTRIBUTION
░ BREEDING
☰ WINTERING

FOOD

The only information on food (available to me) is the late C. G. Harrold's observations in fall on Nunivak Island, off the northwest coast of Alaska. He states these geese fed mostly along the seashore; but occasional flocks were encountered on the tundra, where they were feeding on berries. One adult male specimen had his face stained and his throat and entire intestinal tract dyed blue from a diet of berries.

SOUTHWARD MIGRATION

Harrold recorded the first arrival on August 20 on Nunivak Island, and thereafter Emperor Geese became quite common and remained until he left on October 29. Little other information is available on fall migratory movements.

REFERENCES

Bailey, Alfred M., *The Birds of Cape Prince of Wales, Alaska*, 1943.
Brandt, Herbert, *Alaska Bird Trails*, 1943.
Kortright, Francis H., *The Ducks, Geese and Swans of North America*, 1942.
Swarth, Harry S., *Birds of Nunivak Island, Alaska*, 1934.
The A.O.U. Check-list of North American Birds (Fourth Edition), 1931.

WEIGHTS

Male—*Average of* 5: 6 pounds, 2 ounces. *Extremes:* 5 pounds, 8 ounces to 6 pounds, 12 ounces.

Female—*Average of* 4: 6 pounds, 4 ounces. *Extremes:* 5 pounds, 2 ounces to 6 pounds, 14 ounces.

Emperor Goose

ROSS'S GOOSE

(Chen rossi)

COMMON NAMES

Little Wavy, Galoot, Warty-nosed Wavy.

DESCRIPTION

A diminutive Snow Goose, averaging less than three pounds. All white plumage except for black wing tips. Reddish or purplish bill, the base of which is covered by warty protuberances. Feet—dull red.

Male and female on water. The smallest of North American geese. All white plumage and black wing tips, coupled with small size, are best guides to identification. Rides buoyantly on water. The small, neat head and trim appearance give it a "delicate air," which serves to separate it from its larger relative, the Lesser Snow Goose, with which it sometimes associates on migration. When seen together, the difference in size (the Lesser Snow is twice as large) is conspicuous.

Male and female in flight. The Ross's Goose is much quieter in flight than the garrulous Lesser Snow; but, unless they are seen together when the contrast in size can be readily seen, the small size of Ross's is not so appreciable.

DISTRIBUTION

Winters in the San Joaquin and Sacramento Valleys of California. Migrates through Montana; Alberta (recorded at Many Island Lake, southeastern Alberta; in the Brooks District, south-central; Sullivan Lake, east-central; and the Athabasca Delta, northern Alberta); also at Great Slave Lake in the Northwest Territories. Breeds in the Perry River District, Queen Maud Gulf, Arctic Canada in approximately 67 degrees, 45 minutes north latitude and 102 degrees west longitude. The southward migration follows the same route. Casual in Louisiana, Utah, North Dakota, Manitoba, Saskatchewan, Colorado, Arizona, and Chihuahua.

COURTSHIP AND NESTING

Little is known of the courtship of Ross's Goose. Probably it follows a similar pattern to that of other members of the *Chen* group. The nesting grounds of Ross's Geese were discovered by Angus Gavin and his companion Ernest Donovan in the Perry River District, Queen Maud Gulf, Arctic Canada, on July 1, 1940. The geese were found nesting on stony islands in a narrow lake, which was the source of an unmapped tributary of the Perry. Quoting from Gavin's original narrative, which was published in *The Beaver*, house organ of the Hudson's Bay Company, December, 1940, is the following account: "On the first three islands visited there were about fifty pairs nesting, anywhere from three to thirty feet apart. A grassy base on the rock, copiously lined and rimmed with white down, soiled to a dirty gray appearance, constituted the nest. The complete nest was about twelve inches overall, with a nesting cavity about five inches in diameter and about two and one-half inches in depth from the top of the downy rim. There were two to six creamy-white, ovate eggs in the nests examined. Four eggs were the most common clutch noted." On a subsequent visit (1941), clutches of eight and nine eggs were observed. The eggs measured (average of five) 2.74 by 1.90 inches.

Gavin's Eskimo guides informed him that the principal nesting grounds were on similar islands in a larger lake about six miles away.

HISTORICAL NOTE

Samuel Hearne, in 1795, published a description of the "Horned Wavey" which he encountered on his famous journey to the Coppermine River. It was probably in 1770, the year of his second unsuccessful attempt to reach the Arctic overland, that he encountered "this delicate and diminutive species of the goose . . ." about 200 or 300 miles northwest of Churchill. Nothing more was heard of it until 1861, when Bernard Rogan Ross, a Chief Factor of the Hudson's Bay Company, sent specimens to John Cassin of the Philadelphia Academy of Science, from Fort Resolution, Great Slave Lake, Northwest Territories. Cassin described the bird as a new species and named it *Chen rossi*.

FOOD

Believed to be chiefly vegetable matter. Grazes on the tender shoots of grass during spring migration. Gavin observed them feeding on crowberry (*Empetrum nigrum*) on the tundra.

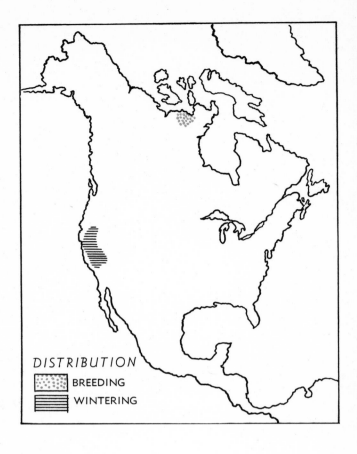

DISTRIBUTION

▚ BREEDING

≣ WINTERING

WEIGHTS

Male—*Average of 18:* 2 pounds, 14 ounces. *Extremes:* 2 pounds, 6 ounces to 3 pounds, 10 ounces.

Female—*Average of 19:* 2 pounds, 11 ounces. *Extremes:* 2 pounds, 5 ounces to 3 pounds, 7 ounces.

REFERENCES

Gavin, Angus, "Birds of Perry River District and Northwest Territories," *Wilson Bulletin*, December, 1947.

——— and Cartwright, "Where the Ross's Geese Nest," *The Beaver*, December, 1940.

Kortright, Francis H., *The Ducks, Geese and Swans of North America*, 1942.

Ross's Goose

SNOW GOOSE

(Chen hyperborea)

COMMON NAMES

White Brant, Wavy, White Wavy, Kang-o-wak (Eskimo).

DESCRIPTION

Two forms of Snow Geese are recognized—Lesser Snow (*C. h. hyperborea*) and Greater Snow (*C .h. atlantica*). Medium and large-sized geese with all-white plumage and black wing tips.

Male and female on water. Snow-white plumage; large size; pink or reddish bill. Black wing tips partially concealed—*inconspicuous.*

Male and female in flight. Snow-white plumage except for *conspicuous* black wing tips. A gray band separates the black primaries from the white part of wing.

DISTRIBUTION

The Lesser Snow breeds in Arctic eastern Siberia and Arctic North America from Point Barrow, Alaska, east to Southampton, the Baffin Islands and islands northward. Winters in Japan and East Asia; in North America chiefly west of the Mississippi (especially California), and on the Gulf coast from Florida to Texas and central Mexico. Casual on the Atlantic coast.

The Greater Snow breeds on northwest Greenland, North Baffin and Ellesmere Islands. Winters on the Atlantic coast from Maryland to North Carolina.

NORTHWARD MIGRATION

In March, the Lesser Snows start northward from the Gulf coast and California. They pause to feed and rest behind the retreating snowline in Iowa, Nebraska, South and North Dakota, Minnesota, Manitoba, Saskatchewan and Alberta. They reach Canada's prairies in late March or early April. The Mississippi Valley contingent is associated with Blue Geese (*C. caerulescens*). They follow a narrow flyline, wedge after wedge. Night and day the air resounds with their excited gabbling. In Manitoba Blues outnumber the Snows. They pass northeastward to Hudson Bay about May 5 to 12 in more or less continuous flights—a spectacular sight. Their Arctic breeding grounds are reached June 1 to 10.

The Greater Snows migrate coastwise along the Atlantic states and concentrate in the Lower St. Lawrence River near Cap Tourmente. They reach their breeding grounds in northwest Greenland about the end of June. They are not numerous but have shown a steady increase for several years, under protection. There are about 20,000 in existence.

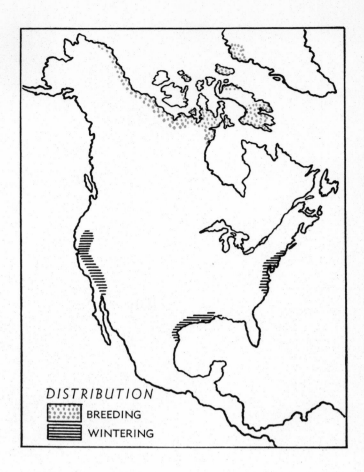

DISTRIBUTION

▦ BREEDING

▤ WINTERING

COURTSHIP AND NESTING

Snow Geese mate for life. The gander guards the incubating female and later assists in caring for the young. Display and posturing are not so elaborate as with ducks. A gander, having made his choice, fiercely repels all rivals; and, when the female joins him in the note of victory, pairing appears to be agreed upon. Display of mutual affection involves head-bobbing and snaky movements of the neck. Lesser Snows nest on dry land (tundra), adjacent to marshy places and small ponds, or on islands. A hollow in the ground among grass or prostrate willow is well lined with grasses, moss, feathers and pale gray down. Four to eight (usually five or six) creamy-white eggs, averaging 3.10 by 2.07 inches, are laid.

Courtship and nesting habits of Greater Snows are similar. The eggs—usually six or seven—average 3.21 by 2.17 inches.

FOOD

On the wintering grounds and on migration Lesser Snows feed on roots and culms of aquatic plants and graze like tame geese on fresh sprouts of cereal and ordinary grasses. In autumn they frequent the stubble fields. Berries, wild rice, aquatic insects and small mollusks are part of the diet. Greater Snows feed on sea cabbage, cord grass and sedges, which they pull up by the roots. Little is known of their feeding habits on the breeding grounds. Ekblaw describes summering birds as feeding at the bottom of shallow ponds in which *Pleuropogon* (Semaphore Grass) and *Hippuris* (Marestail) were abundant.

WEIGHTS

Lesser Snow Male—*Average of 19:* 5 pounds, 5 ounces.
Lesser Snow Female—*Average of 18:* 4 pounds, 11 ounces.
Greater Snow Male—*Average of 19:* 7 pounds, 7 ounces.
Greater Snow Female—*Average of 12:* 6 pounds, 2 ounces.

SOUTHWARD MIGRATION

Lesser Snows appear early in September in the Athabasca Delta, and with Blues at the south end of James Bay. They concentrate on the shallow prairie lakes of Western Canada during October, and the final exodus takes place at freeze-up, usually November 5–15. From James Bay, where they spend most of October, they fly south directly to Louisiana.

Greater Snows leave the breeding grounds early in September and migrate down the Ungava Peninsula to the Lower St. Lawrence River, arriving about September 12. They linger about one month and then head south for Maryland and North Carolina.

REFERENCES

Gavin, Angus, "Birds of Perry River District, Queen Maud Gulf and Arctic Canada," unpublished manuscript, 1943.
Kortright, Francis H., *The Ducks, Geese and Swans of North America,* 1942.
Witherby, Jourdain, Ticehurst and Tucker, *Handbook of British Birds,* 1943.
The A.O.U. Check-list of North American Birds (Fourth Edition), 1931.

Snow Goose

WHITE-FRONTED GOOSE

(Anser albifrons albifrons)

TULE GOOSE

(A. a. gambelli)

COMMON NAMES

Specklebelly, Brant, Nuck-luck (Eskimo).

DESCRIPTION

A grayish-brown goose with orange-yellow legs and feet. White patch around face at base of bill (the White-front); breast and belly variably splashed with black and white, forming incomplete bars. The White-fronted Goose is medium-sized; the Tule Goose is almost as large as the Lesser Canada Goose.

Male and female on water. *All dark brown* goose except for the *white frontal patch around face at base of bill*, and white upper and lower tail coverts. A whitish line divides the sides and closed wings. (Juveniles lack white face patch in first autumn. This is gradually assumed in winter and spring.)

Male and female in flight. Black- and white-splashed breast; white undertail; orange-yellow legs and feet.

DISTRIBUTION

White-fronted Geese breed in the Arctic regions of northeastern Europe and Asia (Siberia eastward) to North America and the west coast of Greenland. In North America, from the Yukon Valley east to Anderson River, Clinton Colden Lake, Mackenzie and the Perry River District and Queen Maud Gulf. Winters in southern Europe and Asia, and (in America) from southern British Columbia and southern Illinois south to Louisiana, Texas and Mexico.

Tule Geese were found breeding on islands in a fresh-water lake in the Perry River District and in Queen Maud Gulf in 1941 by Angus Gavin. They kept strictly apart from the smaller White-fronted Geese, which were also nesting in nearby lakes. They occur in fall migration at the Pas, Manitoba, and at Neilburg, Saskatchewan; but no scientific specimens are yet preserved in Canadian institutions. They winter in the Sacramento Valley, California.

NORTHWARD MIGRATION

White-fronts migrate in March and April from the wintering grounds. By the middle of May they are on the breeding grounds in the Hooper Bay region, Alaska—according to Brandt—and in the Perry River District around Queen Maud Gulf by June 1, according to Gavin.

The Tule Geese probably migrate through Alberta, Canada, with the Lesser Canada Geese; but so far their migration has not been established.

COURTSHIP AND NESTING

Courtship takes place in winter and mating is for life. As is the habit of geese, a courting gander acts fiercely toward all rivals, drives them off with much ado and hurries back to his lady love uttering a "triumph note." The female shows little interest at first but later apparently signifies her acceptance of his suit when she joins him in giving the "triumph note."

The nest is a depression on dry land in a clump of grass, found in various situations from the flats to the uplands. In the Perry River District, islands in freshwater lakes are preferred nesting sites; but some nests are found on the tundra. The five to seven white eggs, which become nest-stained as incubation progresses, are laid one every other day (usually), and down is added copiously toward the end of the incubation period, which is about 28 days. The nest is made of grasses, moss and rootlets. The White-front's eggs measure 3.11 by 2.07 inches (average). The egg measurements of the Tule Goose are unknown.

FOOD

Food consists chiefly of vegetable matter: the tender shoots of grasses, cereal and other grains, berries, beechnuts and acorns. The small quantity of animal matter comprises aquatic larvae, insects and snails. White-fronts are rated top quality for the table.

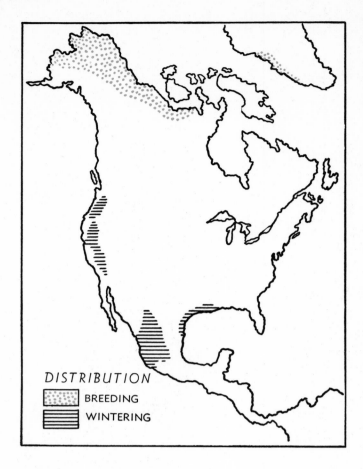

DISTRIBUTION

▨ BREEDING

▤ WINTERING

SOUTHWARD MIGRATION

White-fronts and Tule Geese are western species found chiefly in the central and Pacific flyways. They appear on the western Canadian plains in October in company with Canada and Lesser Snow Geese. White-fronts are relatively rare in Manitoba at the south end of Lake Manitoba but become increasingly numerous west through Saskatchewan and Alberta. The migration routes of the Tule Goose are not known but probably lie chiefly through Alberta to its winter home in northern California.

WEIGHTS

White-front Male—*Average of 21 : 5 pounds, 5 ounces.*
White-front Female—*Average of 17 : 4 pounds, 13 ounces.*
Tule Male—*Average of 16 : 6 pounds, 11 ounces.*
Tule Female—*Average of 12 : 5 pounds, 10 ounces.*

REFERENCES

Brandt, Herbert, *Alaska Bird Trails*, 1943.
Kortright, Francis H., *The Ducks, Geese and Swans of North America*, 1942.
Witherby, Jourdain, Ticehurst and Tucker, *Handbook of British Birds*, 1943.
The A.O.U. Check-list of North American Birds (Fourth Edition), 1931.

White-fronted Goose